"Black & White" Parliamentary Album, 1895

'Black & White"

PARLIAMENTARY A.

1895

PRINTED AND PUBLISHED BY

THE BLACK AND WHITE PUBLISHING COMPANY

63, FLEET STREET, LONDON, E.C.

LONDON:
PRINTED BY THE BLACK AND WHITE PUBLISHING CO.
34, BOUVERIE STREET, E.C.

THE CABINET

THE RT. HON. LORD HALSBURY
Lord Chancellor

THE RT. HON. THE DUKE OF
DEVONSHIRE
Lord President of the Council

THE RT

THE R.T. HON. EARL CADOGAN
Irish Viceroy

THE RIGHT HON. LORD JAMES
Chancellor of the Duchy

THE RT
C

THE RT. HON. LORD ASHBOURNE
Irish Lord Chancellor

**THE RT. HON. LORD BALFOUR
OF BURLEIGH**
Scottish Secretary

*The othe
are in the (
under the (*

RT. HO!

     ,,

     :,

     ,,

     ,,

     :,

     ,,

     ,,

     ,,

     ,,

UNIVERSITIES

Cambridge University

. HON. SIR J. E. GORST, Q.C. (C)

1895—Unopposed
1892—Unopposed
Representation Unchanged

Cambridge University

PROFESSOR R. C. JEBB (C)

1895—Unopposed
1892—Unopposed
Representation Unchanged

Dublir

RT. HON. D. R.

1895—Unopposed
1892—Rt Hon D. R.
E. H. Carson (
Col. Corry Low
Represent:

Dublin University

MR. E. H. CARSON, Q.C. (C)

1895—Unopposed
1892—Unopposed
Representation Unchanged

Edinburgh & St. Andrews Universities

SIR C. J. PEARSON (C)

1895—Unopposed
1892—Unopposed
Representation Unchanged

Glasg

MR.

London University

T. HON. SIR JOHN LUBBOCK (LU)

1895—Unopposed

1892—Unopposed

Representation Unchanged

Oxford University

RT. HON. SIR J. R. MOWBRAY (C)

1895—Unopposed

1892—Unopposed

Representation Unchanged

Oxfo

MR. J

18

18

Represe

Battersea
MR. JOHN BURNS (R)

1895—John Burns (R)	..	5019
C. R. Smith (C)	..	4766
Majority	..	253
1892—Burns (R)	..	5616
Chinnery (C)	..	4057
Majority	..	1559
Representation Unchanged		

Bethnal Green (North-East)
MR. M. BHOWNAGGREE (C)

1895—M. Bhownaggree (C)	..	2591
G. Howell (R)	..	2431
Majority	..	160
1892—Howell (R)	..	2898
Marks (C)	..	2321
Taylor (Lab)	..	106
Ballard (Ind)	..	23
Majority	..	577
Conservative Gain		

Bet
MR.

1895—E. H	
W. A	
1892—Picke	
Bens	

Camberwell (Dulwich)

SIR J. BLUNDELL MAPLE (C)

95—Sir J. B. Maple (C)	.. .. ..	..	5258
C. G. Clarke (R)	.. .. ..	..	2176
	Majority	.. ..	3082
2—Maple (C) ..	.. .. ..	..	5318
Clayden (R)	.. .. ..	..	3138
	Majority	.. ..	2180
	Representation Unchanged		

Camberwell (North)

MAJOR DALBIAC (C)

1895—Major Dalbiac (C) ..	.. .. ..	..	4009
E. H. Bayley (R)	.. .. ..	..	3316
Palmer (Ind)	.. .. ..	..	32
	Majority	.. .. ..	693
1892—Bayley (R)	.. .. ..	..	4295
Kelly (C) ..	—	..	3450
	Majority	.. .. ..	845
	Conservative Gain		

Camber...

MR. F. G...

1895—F. G. Banbu...		
C. Clements (		
	M...	
1892—Banbury (C)	..	
Jones (R) ..		
Ellis (Lab)..		
	M...	
	Represe...	

Chelsea

MR. C. A. WHITMORE (C)

1895—C. A. Whitmore (C) 5524
     O. Beatty (R) 3604

        Majority 1920

1892—Whitmore (C) 4993
     Costelloe (R) 4427

        Majority 566
    Representation Unchanged

City of London

MR. A. G. H. GIBBS (C)

1895—Unopposed

1892—Sir R. Hanson (C) 10556
     A. G. H. Gibbs (C) 9258
     Alderman Ritchie (C) 4207

        Majority 6349
    Representation Unchanged

S

1895—Unop

1892—Sir R.
     A. G.
     Alder

Clapham

Croydon

MR. P. M. THORNTON (C)

95—P. M. Thornton (C)	..	..	..	..	5925
J. Kempster (R)	..	..	..	..	3904
Majority	..	..	..	..	2021
92—Thornton (C)	..	..	..	..	5170
McKenna (R) ..	..	..	..	..	4526
Majority	..	..	..	..	6;4

Representation Unchanged

THE RT. HON. C. T. RITCHIL (C)

1895—The Rt Hon C. T. Ritchie (C)	..	..	6876
C. C. Hutchinson (R)	..	..	..	4647
Majority	..	..	..	2229
1892—Herbert (C)	..	..	..	6528
Grimwade (R) ..	..	..	..	4834
Majority	..	..	..	1694

Representation Unchanged

MR. C. J. DA

1895—C. J. Darling (	
T. Macnamara	
Majc	
1892—Darling (C)	
Fitzmaurice (R	
Maj	

Represent

Finsbury (Central)

HON. W. F. MASSEY-MAINWARING (C)

1895—W. F. Massey-Mainwaring (C)		3588
D. Naoroji (R)		2783
Majority		805
189ε—Naoroji (R)		2959
Penton (C)..		2956
Majority		3
Conservative Gain		

Finsbury (East)

MR. H. C. RICHARDS (C)

1895—H. Richards (C)		2260
J. Rowlands (R)		1990
Majority		270
1892—Rowlands (R)		2383
Shadwell (C)		2093
Majority		ɔ90
Conservative Gain		

SIR CE

1895—Unop
1892—Gains
2477:
1892)-

Fulham

MR. W. HAYES FISHER (C)

1895—W. H. Fisher (C)	..	..	..	..	..	5378
E. A. Cornwall (R)	..	..	..	..	..	3915
W. Parnell (Lab)	..	..	..	..	..	191
	Majority	..	..	..	..	1463
1892—Fisher (C)	..	..	..	..	..	4365
Barnett (R)	..	..	..	..	..	4154
	Majority	..	..	..	..	211
	Representation Unchanged					

Greenwich

LORD H. CECIL (C)

1895—Lord H. Cecil (C)	..	..	..	..	..	4802
G. C. Whiteley (R)	..	..	..	..	..	3564
	Majority	..	..	..	..	1238
1892—Boord (C)	..	..	..	..	..	4200
Whiteley (R)	..	..	..	..	..	3877
	Majority	..	..	..	..	323
	Representation Unchanged					

Hac

SIR A. R.

1895—Sir A. R. Sc			
C. Russell (I			
	M		
1892—Scoble (C)	..		
Stewart (R)			
	M		
	Repres		

Hackney (North)
MR. W. R. BOUSFIELD, Q.C. (C)

1895—W. R. Bousfield (C)	.. ..	4725
S. Mayer (R)	.. ..	2460
	Majority	2265
1892—Bousfield (C)	.. ..	4799
McCall (R)	.. ..	3280
	Majority	1519

Representation Unchanged

Hackney (South)
MR. T. H. ROBERTSON (C)

1895—T. H. Robertson (C)	.. .. ..	4681
J. F. Moulton, Q.C. (R)	.. .. ..	4362
	Majority	319

1892—Sir Charles Russell (R), 4440 ; Robertson (C),
3294 ; Majority, 1146. Bye-election (May,
1894)—J. F. Moulton (R), 4530 ; Robertson
(C), 4338 ; Majority, 192.

Conservative Gain

MAJOR-GE

1895—Maj.-Ge
W. C. St

1892—

Hampstead

MR. E. BRODIE HOARE (C)

1895—Unopposed

1892—Brodie Hoare (C) 3848
    Hanham (R) 2239

         Majority 1609
    Representation Unchanged

Islington (East)

MR. B. L. COHEN (C)

1895—B. L. Cohen (C) 4383
    T. McKinnon Wood (R) .: 3159

         Majority 1224

1892—Cohen (C) 3975
    Bunting (R) 3510

         Majority 465
    Representation Unchanged

Is

MR. G.

1895—G. C. Bart
    Dr. Napier

1892—Bartley (C
    Hill (R)

        Repr

Islington (South)

SIR ALBERT KAYE ROLLIT (C)

1895—Sir A. K. Rollit (C)	..	..	..	..	3563
Dr. H. Hart (R)	..	..	..	..	2342
	Majority	..	..	..	1221
1892—Rollit (C)	..	..	..	..	3124
Digby (R)	..	..	..	..	2673
	Majority	..	..	..	421
	Representation Unchanged				

Islington (West)

MR. T. LOUGH (R)

1895—T. Lough (R)	..	..	..	..	3494
G. Barham (LU)	..	..	..	..	3031
	Majority	..	..	..	463
1892—Lough (R)	..	..	..	..	3385
R. Chamberlain (LU)	..	..	..	2655
	Majority	..	..	..	730
	Representation Unchanged				

MR. W

1895—W. E.			
F. C.			
1892—Frye (...			
Sharpe			

Kensington (South)
SIR ALGERNON BORTHWICK (C)

1895—Unopposed
1892—Unopposed
Representation Unchanged

Lambeth (Brixton)
LORD CARMARTHEN (C)

1895—Carmarthen, Marquis of (C)	.. ..	4198
Sir R. G. Head (R)	.. .. ..	2199
Majority	.. ., ...	1999
1892—Carmarthen (C)	.. .. ..	4061
Stapley (R)	.. ..	3204
Majority	.. .. ..	857

Representation Unchanged

L
MI

1895—F. L. C
M. H.
W. Wi

1892—Beaufo
Hegg (

Lambeth (North)

MR. H. M. STANLEY (LU)

1895—H. M. Stanley (LU)	..	..	..	..	2873
C. P. Trevelyan (R)	..	.:	..	..	2477
	Majority	..	..	..	401
1892—Coldwells (R)	..	..	..	..	2524
Stanley (LU)	..	..	..	..	2394
	Majority	..	..	..	130
	Liberal Unionist Gain			

Lambeth (Norwood)

MR. CHARLES ERNEST TRITTON

1895—Unopposed				
1892—Mr. C. E. Tritton (C)	..	..	..	..	4147
Dr. Verdon (R)	..	..	..	..	2584
	Majority	..	..	..	1563
	Representation Unchanged			

MR.

1895—Unopposed

1892—Mr. J. Pe
Harvey (N

Rep

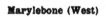

Marylebone (East)	**Marylebone (West)**
MR. E. BOULNOIS (C)	SIR H. FARQUHAR, BART. (C)

Newingto

MR. J.

1895—E. Boulnois (C) 3379
    Col. A. Gardner (R) 1845

        Majority 1534

1892—Boulnois (C) 3122
    G. Whale (R) 2300

        Majority 822
    Representation Unchanged

1895—Sir H. Farquhar (C) 3734
    B. Strauss (R) 2273

        Majority 1461

1892—Seager-Hunt (C) 2913
    Foulgar (R) 2476

        Majority 437
    Representation Unchanged

1895—J. Bailey (C) ..
    R. Spokes (R) ..
    G. Lansbury (S

        Majo

1892—Saunders (R),
    Majority, 296.
    Bailey (C), 2676
    571.
      Representa

Newington (West)

CAPTAIN C. W. NORTON (R)

1895—Captain Norton (R)	3219
G. W. Tallents (C)	2769
Majority	450
1892—Norton (R)	3421
Tallents (C)	2328
Majority	1093
Representation Unchanged	

Paddington (North)

MR. JOHN AIRD (C)

1895—J. Aird (C)	2894
G. H. Maberly (R)	1852
Majority	1042
1892—Aird (C)	2591
Terrell (R)	2281
Majority	310
Representation Unchanged	

Pad

MR. T.

1
In 1892 the Di
Randolph Church
Right Hon. Mer
returned without
representation.

Repres

St. George's, Hanover Square

THE RT. HON. G. J. GOSCHEN (C)

1895—Unopposed
1892—Unopposed
Representation Unchanged

St. Pancras (East)

MR. R. G. WEBSTER (C)

1895—R. G. Webster (C)	..	..	..	..	2612
B. F. Costelloe (R)	..	..	..	..	2323
	Majority	..	..	..	289
1892—Webster (C)	..	..	..	..	2621
Gibb (R)	..	..	..	..	2180
	Maj rity	..	..	..	441

Representation Unchanged

St. P

MR. E. I

1895—E. R. P. Moc
H. H. Rapha
J. Leighton (

Ma

1892—Bolton (R, su
Meon (C) ..
Leighton (Ir.c

Ma
Represe

St. Pancras (South)	St. Pancras (West)	Shoredit
SIR J. GOLDSMID, BART. (LU)	MR. H. R. GRAHAM (C)	MR. J.

St. Pancras (South)

SIR J. GOLDSMID, BART. (LU)

1895—Sir J. Goldsmid (LU) 2433
G. M. Harris (R) 1223

Majority 1210

1892—Goldsmid (LU) 2470
Beale (R) 2033

Majority 437
Representation Unchanged

St. Pancras (West)

MR. H. R. GRAHAM (C)

1895—H. R. Graham (C).. 3104
Dr. W. J. Collins (R) 2273

Majority 831

1892—Graham (C) 2984
Lawson (R) 2942

Majority 42
Representation Unchanged

Shoredit

MR. J.

1895—J. Lowles (C) .. ..
W. R. Creme

Ma

1892—Cremer (R) .. ..
Firbank (C)

Ma
Cor

Shoreditch (Hoxton)	Southwark (Bermondsey)	Sout
PROFESSOR J. STUART (R)	MR. A. LAFONE (C)	MR. J.

1895—J. Stuart (R) 2990
Hon C. G. Hay (C) 2862

     Majority 128

1892—Stuart (R).. 3410
Hay (C) 2114
Donald (Lab) 19

     Majority 1296
   Representation Unchanged

1895—A. Lafone (C) 4182
R. V. Barrow (R) 3822

     Majority 360

1892—Barrow (R) 4390
Lafone (C).. 3732

     Majority 658
     Conservative Gain

1895—J. C. Ma
A. Pome

1892—Macdona
Glanville

     Rep

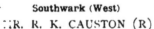

Southwark (West)	Strand	Tower
MR. R. K. CAUSTON (R)	THE HON. W. F. D. SMITH (C)	HON.

Southwark (West)

MR. R. K. CAUSTON (R)

1895—R. K. Causton (R) ..	..	..	..	2989
F. Horner (C) ..	..	..	..	2870
Majority	..	..	..	119
1892—Causton (R)	..	..	..	3534
Bond (C) ..	..	..	..	2295
Majority	..	..	..	1239

Representation Unchanged

Strand

THE HON. W. F. D. SMITH (C)

1895—Unopposed
1892—Unopposed

Representation Unchanged

Tower

HON.

1895—Hon I
J. N.

1892—Macdo
Colom

Tower Hamlets (Limehouse)	Tower Hamlets (Mile End)	
MR. H. S. SAMUEL (C)	**MR. SPENCER CHARRINGTON (C)**	**MR. S**

Tower Hamlets (Limehouse)

MR. H. S. SAMUEL (C)

1895—H. S. Samuel (C)	2661
W. M. Thompson (R)	2071
Majority	590
1892—Wallace (R)	2475
Samuel (C)	2305
Majority	170
Conservative Gain	

Tower Hamlets (Mile End)

MR. SPENCER CHARRINGTON (C)

1895—Charrington (C)	2383
Haysman (R)	1516
Majority	867
1892—Charrington (C)	2204
Haysman (R)	1931
Majority	273
Representation Unchanged	

MR. S

1895—S. C.
W. F
1892—Buxt
Welb

Tower Hamlets (St. George's in the East)	Tower Hamlets (Stepney)	Tower Ha
MR. H. MARKS (C)	MR. F. W. ISAACSON (C)	SIR S. MON

Tower Hamlets (St. George's in the East)

MR. H. MARKS (C)

1895—H. Marks (C)	1583
G. W. Benn (R)	1579
Majority	4
1892—Benn (R)	1661
Ritchie (C)	1263
Majority	398
Conservative Gain	

Tower Hamlets (Stepney)

MR. F. W. ISAACSON (C)

1895—F. W. Isaacson (C)..	2348
W. H. Dickinson (R)	1876
Majority	472
1892—Isaacson (C)	2298
Thompson (R)	2203
Majority	95
Representation Unchanged	

Tower Ha

SIR S. MON

1895—Sir S. Monta	
Sir W. H. Po	
M	
1892—Montagu (R	
Poer-Trench	
M	
Represe	

Wandsworth
MR. H. KIMBER (C)

1895—H. Kimber (C)..	6482
M. Mayhew (R)	3248
Majority	3234
1892—Kimber (C)	5913
Crook (R)	3690
Majority	2223
Representation Unchanged	

West Ham (North)
MR. E. GRAY (C)

1895—E. Gray (C)	5635
T. N. A. Grove (R)	4931
Majority	704
1892—Grove (R)	4974
Forrest Fulton (C)	4943
Majority	31
Conservative Gain	

MA

1895—Major
J. Kei

1892—Keir I
Banes

Westminster

MR. W. L. BURDETT-COUTTS (C)

1895—Unopposed

1892—W. L. Burdett-Coutts (C) 3540
     L. S. Jones (R) 1910
                                 —————
           Majority 1630

Woolwich

COLONEL HUGHES (C)

1895—Col. Hughes (C) .. ..
     B. Jones (Lab) .. ..

           Majority .. .. ..

1892—Hughes (C) .. ..
     Jones (Lab) .. ..

           Majority .. ..
Representation Unchanged

Ashton-under-Lyne

MR. H. WHITELEY (C)

1895—H. Whiteley (C)	3434
W. Woods (R)	2680
J. Sexton (Lab)	415
Majority	754
1892—Addison (C)	3358
Morgan (R)	3223
Majority	135

Representation Unchanged

Aston Manor

CAPT. G. W. GRICE-HUTCHINSON (C)

1895—Captain Grice-Hutchinson (C)	5253
J. Lawson (Temp)	1075
Majority	3678
1892—Grice-Hutchinson (C)	5300
Ward (Lab)	1313
Majority	3987

Representation Unchanged

Ba

MR. C

1895—C. W. Cay
W. C. Bor
P. Curran
1892—Cayzer (C)
Duncan (F

Repr

Bath

COL. C. WYNDHAM MURRAY (C)

1895—Col. C. W. Murray (C) 3445
    E. R. Wodehouse (LU).. 3358
    Sir W. M. Conway (R).. 2917
    J. M. Fuller (R) 2865

           Majority 528

1892—Murray (C) 3198
    Wodehouse (LU) 3177
    Baptie (R).. 2981
    Adye (R) 2941

           Majority 217
    Representation Unchanged

Bath

MR. E. R. WODEHOUSE (LU)

1895—Colonel Murray (C) 3445
    E. R. Wodehouse (LU) 3358
    Sir W. M. Conway (R) 2917
    J. M. Fuller (R) 2865

           Majority 441

1892—Murray (C), 3198; Wodehouse (LU), 3177;
    Baptie (R), 2981; Adye (R), 2941: Majority,
    196

    Representation Unchanged

1895—C. G.
    S. H.

1892—Whitb
    Pym (

Birkenhead

MR. ELLIOTT LEES (C)

1895—E. Lees (C) 6178
W. H. Lever (R) 5974

Majority 204

1892—Lord Bury (C). 5763; W. H. Lever (R), 5156:
Majority, 604. Bye-Election (October, 1894)
Lees (C), 6149; Lever (R), 6043: Majority,
106

Representation Unchanged

Birmingham (Bordesley)

RT. HON. JESSE COLLINGS (LU)

1895—Rt Hon Jesse Collings (LU) 6004
Alderman Cook (R) 2154

Majority 3850

1892—Collings (LU) 6380
Davis (Lab) 2658

Majority 3722
Representation Unchanged

Bi

MR. EBE

1895—Unoppo

1892—John All
J. Herb

Re

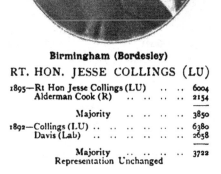

Birmingham (East)
SIR BENJAMIN STONE (C)

1895—Unopposed
1892—Rt Hon H. Matthews (C) 5041
 Fulford (R) 2832
 Collin (Temp) 296
 —
 Majority 2209
 Representation Unchanged

Birmingham (Edgbaston)
MR. G. DIXON (LU)

1895—Unopposed
1892—Unopposed
Representation Unchanged

MR.

1895—W.
 W.

1892—Ke
 Blo

Birmingham (South)

MR. J. POWELL WILLIAMS (LU)

1895—J. Powell Williams (LU)	.. .. ..	4830
W. Priestman (R)	.. ..	1257
	Majority	3573
1892—Williams (LU) ..	.. .. ..	5193
Lancaster (R)	.. ..	2270
	Majority	2923
	Representation Unchanged	

Birmingham (West)

RT. HON. JOSEPH CHAMBERLAIN (LU)

1895—Rt Hon J. Chamberlain (LU)	.. ..	5537
Dr. B. O'Connor (R)	.. .. ..	1259
	Majority	4278
1892—Chamberlain (LU) ..	.. .. ..	6297
Corrie Grant (R)	.. ..	1879
Mahoney (Ind)	.. ..	31
	Majority	4418
	Representation Unchanged	

MR. W.

1895—W. H.	
W. Cod	
T. P. R	

1892—Hornby	
Coddin	
Taylor (	
Heywor	

R

Blackburn

MR. W. H. HORNBY (C)

1895—W. H. Hornby (C)	..	..	..	..	..	9553
W. Coddington (C)		..	..	..	..	9150
T. P. Ritzema (R)	..	..	..	..	..	6840
	Majority	..	..	..	..	2713
1892—Hornby (C)	..	..	..	..	..	9265
Coddington (C)	..	..	..	..	..	9046
Taylor (R)	..	..	..	..	..	7272
Heyworth (R)	..	..	..	..	..	6694
	Majority	..	..	..	..	1993

Representation Unchanged

Bolton

MR. H. SHEPHERD CROSS (C)

1895—H. S. Cross (C)	..	..	..	..	8494
G. Harwood (R)		..	..	..	8453
Colonel Hon F. C. Bridgman (C)		..	7901
F. Brocklehurst (Lab)	..	..	..	7694
	Majority	..	..	..	41
1892—Cross (C)	..	..	..	..	8429
Bridgman (C)	..	..	..	..	8140
Taylor (R)	..	..	..	..	7575
Harwood (R)	..	..	..	..	7536
	Majority	..	..	..	854

Radical Gain of One

MR.

1895—H. S. C			
G. Har			
Colonel			
Brockle			
1892—Cross (C			
Bridgm			
Taylor			
Harwo			

Boston

MR. W. GARFIT (C)

1895—W. Garfit (C)	..	..	..	..	1633
Sir W. J. Ingram (R)	..	..	..	..	1237
	Majority	..	..	..	396
1892—Ingram (R)	..	..	..	..	1355
Lord Willoughby (C)	..	..	..	..	1313
	Majority	..	..	..	42
	Conservative Gain				

Bradford (Central)

MR. J. L. WANKLYN (LU)

1895—J. L. Wanklyn (LU)	..	..	..	4024
Rt Hon G. J. Shaw Lefevre (R)	..	3983
	Majority	..	..	..	41
1892—Shaw Lefevre (R)	..	..	..	4710
Marquis of Lorne (LU)	..	..	..	4245
	Majority	..	..	..	465
	Liberal Unionist Gain				

MR. H.

1895—H. B. Re			
W. S. Ca			
1892—Caine (R			
Reed (C)			

Bradford (West)

MR. ERNEST FLOWER (C)

1895—E. Flower (C)	.. ..	3936
J. C. Horsfall (R)	.. .. ..	3481
Ben Tillett (Lab)	.. ..	2364
	Majority	.. .. ..	455
1892—Illingworth (R)	.. ..	3306
Flower (C)	.. ..	3053
Ben Tillet (Lab)	.. ..	2749
	Majority	.. .. ..	253

Conservative Gain

Brighton

MR. B. C. V. WENTWORTH (C)

1895—G. Loder (C) 7878
B. C. V. Wentworth (C) 7493
Sir J. Ewart (R) 5082

Majority 2411

1892—Loder (C), 7807; Marriott (C), 7134; F. W.
Maude (R), 5448: Majority, 2359. Bye-
election (Dec., 1893)—Wentworth returned
unopposed.

Representation Unchanged

M

1895—G. Lod
B. C. W
Sir J.

1892—Loder (
(R), 5
(Dec.,
posed

R

Bristol (East)
SIR. W. H. WILLS (R)

1895—Sir W. H. Wills (R) **4129**
     S. G. Hobson (Lab) **1874**

        Majority **2255**

1892—Weston (R) unopposed. Bye-election (March, 1895)—Wills (R), 3740 ; Gore (Lab), 3558 : Majority, 182.

     Representation Unchanged

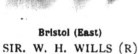

Bristol (North)
MR. LEWIS FRY (LU)

1895—L. Fry (LU) **4702**
     G. Townsend (R) **4464**

        Majority **238**

1892—Townsend (R) **4409**
     Fry (LU) **4064**

        Majority **345**
     Liberal Unionist Gain

SIR EDV

1895—Sir E. S. F
     J. O'Conn

1892—Hill (C)
     Fry (R)

     Repr

Bristol (West)
RT. HON. SIR M. HICKS-BEACH (C)

1895—The Rt Hon Sir M. Hicks-Beach (C).. 3815
    H. Lawless (R)   1842

         Majority   1973

1892—Hicks-Beach Unopposed
     Representation Unchanged

Burnley
HON. P. J. STANHOPE (R)

1895—P. J. Stanhope (R)..   5454
    W. A. Lindsay (C)..   5133
    H. M. Hyndman (Soc)   1498

         Majority   321

1892—J. S. Balfour (R), 6450; Lawrence (LU),
     5035: Majority, 1415. Bye-election (Feb.,
     1893) — Stanhope (R), 6199; Lindsay (C),
     5506: Majority, 693
     Representation Unchanged

MR.

1895—J. Kenyon
    J. F. Che

1892—Sir H. Ja
    Parks (R

         Rep

Bury St. Edmunds
VISCOUNT CHELSEA (C)

1895—Unopposed

1892—Lord F. Hervey (C), 1267; Major Jameson
(R), 863: Majority, 404. Bye-election
(Aug., 1892)—Viscount Chelsea Unopposed.

Representation Unchanged

Cambridge
MR. PENROSE FITZGERALD (C)

1895—R. P. Fitzgerald (C)	..	..	..	..	3574
A. J. David (R)	..	..	..	..	2920
Majority	..	..	..	..	654
1892—Fitzgerald (C) ..	..	..	..	..	3299
R. C. Lehmann (R)	..	..	..	..	3044
Majority	..	..	..	..	255

Representation Unchanged

MR. J. H

R

Carlisle

RT. HON. W. C. GULLY, Q.C. (R)

1895—W. C. Gully (R)	.. ..	3167
S. P. Foster (C)	.. ..	2853
	Majority	.. .. ..	314
1892—Gully (R) ..	.. ..	2729
Foster (C) ..	.. ..	2586
	Majority	.. .. ..	143
	Representation Unchanged		

Chatham

MR. H. D. DAVIES (C)

1895—H. D. Davies (C)	.. ..	4082
R. H. Cox (R)..	.. ..	3499
	Majority	.. .. ..	583
1892—Lloyd (C) ..	.. ..	3777
Clarke (R)..	.. ..	3400
	Majority	.. .. ..	377
	Representation Unchanged		

COLONE

1895—Colonel
W. Blay
Hillen (I

1892—Agg-Gar
Debenha

Re

Chester

MR. R. A. YERBURGH (C)

5—Unopposed

2—Yerburgh (C) 3148
  Baron Halkett (R) 2528

  Majority 620
  Representation Unchanged

Christchurch

MR. A. H. SMITH (C)

1895—A. H. Smith (C) 3198
  Hon. T. A. Brassey (R) 3144

  Majority 54

1892—Smith (C) 2803
  Fletcher (R) 2600

  Majority 203
  Representation Unchanged

SIR W.

1895—Sir W.
  E. S. N

1892—Captain
  (R , 21
  1895) —
  2296: N
  R

Coventry

MR. CHAS. JAMES MURRAY (C)

1895—C. J. Murray (C) 4974
      W. H. Ballantine (R) 4624

         Majority 350

1892—Ballantine (R) 4754
      Murray (C) 4611

         Majority 143
      Conservative Gain

Darlington

MR. ARTHUR PEASE (LU)

1895—A. Pease (LU) 3354
      Sir T. Fry, Bart. (R) 2697

         Majority 657

1892—Fry (R) 2866
      Pease (LU) 2810

         Majority 56
      Unionist Gain

MR.

1895—H. Bemro
      G. Drage
      Rt Hon Si
      Sir T. Ro

1892—Harcourt
      (C), 5546
      1961. By
      (R), 6508
      Majority,
        Cons

Derby

MR. GEOFFREY DRAGE (C)

1895—H. Bemrose (C) 7907
G. Drage (C) 7076
Rt Hon Sir W. V. Harcourt (R) .. 6785
Sir T. Roe (R).. 6475

Majority 291

1892—Harcourt (R), 7507; Roe (R), 7389; Hextall
(C), 5546; Haslam (LU), 5363; Majority,
1961. Bye-election (Aug., 1892)—Harcourt
(R), 6508; Farmer-Atkinson (C), 1619;
Majority, 4889
Conservative Gain of Two

Devonport

MR. H. E. KEARLEY (R)

1895—H. E. Kearley (R).. 3570
E. J. C. Morton (R) 3511
P. Wippell (LU) 3303
Captain T. Thynne (C).. 3263

Majority 267

1892—Kearley (R) 3354
Morton (R) 3325
Price (C) 3012
Harvey (C) 2972

Majority 342
Representation Unchanged

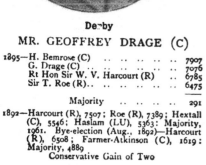

MR.

1895—M. Old
H. S. C
E. R. H

1892—Oldroy
Cautley

R

Dover

MR. GEORGE WYNDHAM (C)

1895—Unopposed

1892—G. Wyndham (C) 2231
    Edwards (R) 978

        Majority 1253
    Representation Unchanged

Dudley

MR. BROOKE ROBINSON (C)

1895—R. B. Robinson (C) 6536
    C. J. Fleming, Q.C. (R) 5795

        Majority 741
1892—Robinson (C) 6668
    H. Spensley (R) 5619

        Majority 1049
    Representation Unchanged

MR. MAT

1895—M. Fowle
    Hon A. H

1892—Fowler (F
    Milvain (

        Rep

Exeter

SIR H. S. NORTHCOTE (C)

95—Sir H. S. Northcote (C) 3857
A. S. Hogg (R) 3363

Majority 494

)2—Northcote (C) 3884
Dunn (R) 3329

Majority 555
Representation Unchanged

Falmouth and Penryn

MR. F. J. HORNIMAN (R)

1895—F. J. Horniman (R) 1150
W. G. Cavendish Bentinck (C) 1101

Majority 49

1892—C. Bentinck (C) 1218
Serena (R).. 880

Majority 338
Radical Gain

MR. W

1895—W. Alla
J. Lucas

1892—James (F
293. By
(R), 6434

Re

Gloucester

MR. C. J. MONK (LU)

1895—C. J. Monk (LU)	3264
S. Wells (R)	2791
Majority	473
1892—Robinson (R)	2885
Monk (LU)	2800
Majority	85
Liberal Unionist Gain	

Grantham

MR. H. Y. B. LOPES (C)

1895—H. Y. B. Lopes (C)	1507
S. D. Waddy, Q.C. (R)	1167
Majority	340
1892—Lopes (C)	1296
Clarke (R)..	126;
Majority	36
Representation Unchanged	

MR. J.

1895—J. D. Palm	
L. M. Joh	
1892—Palmer (C	
Shipman (	
Repr	

Grimsby

MR. G. DOUGHTY (R)

1895—G. Doughty (R) **4347**
Rt Hon E. Heneage (LU) 4166
                                    ———
            Majority 181

1892—Josse (R), 4201; Heneage (LU), 3565;
Ma·ority, 636. Bye-Election (March, 1893)
—Heneage (LU), 4427; Broadhurst (L),
3463; Majority, 964
            Radical Gain

Halifax

MR. ALFRED ARNOLD (C)

1895—A. Arnold (C) 5475
W. R. Shaw (R) 5085
J. Booth (R) 4283
J. Lister (Lab).. 3818
                                ———
            Majority 390

1892—Shaw (R), 6581; Stansfeld (R), 6461; Arnold
(C), 4663: Majority, 1918. Bye-election
(Feb., 1893)—Shaw (R), 4620; Arnold (C).
1251; Lister (Lab), 3028: Majority, 369
            Conservative Gain

MR. W

1895—A. Arnold
W. R. Sha
J. Booth (
J. Lister (

1892—Shaw (R),
(C), 4663
1893)—Sh
Lister (La

Hanley
MR. WILLIAM WOODALL (R)

1895—W. Woodall (R)	..	..	..	..	..	5653
A. H. Heath (C)	..	..	..	..	..	5367
	Majority	..	..	..	..	286
1892—Woodall (R)	..	..	..	..	..	5825
Heath (C)	..	..	..	..	..	3992
	Majority	..	..	..	..	1833

Representation Unchanged

Hartlepool
MR. T. RICHARDSON (LU)

1895—T. Richardson (LU)	..	..	..	..	4853
Sir C. Furness, Bart. (R)	..	..	..	4772
	Majority	..	..	..	..	81
1892—Furness (R)	..	..	..	..	..	4626
Richardson (LU)	..	..	..	..	4550
	Majority	..	..	..	..	76

Liberal Unionist Gain

MR.

1895—W.	
C.	
1892—No	
He	

Hereford

MR. C. W. R. COOKE (C)

1895—C. W. R. Cooke (C) 1669
    Sir E. D. Pearce Edgcumbe (R) .. 1356

        Majority 313

1892—Grenfell (R), 1507; Sir J. R. Bailey (C), 1380:
Majority, 127. Bye-election (1893)—C. W.
R. Cooke (C), 1504 ; Sir J. Pulley (R), 1460 :
Majority, 44.
    Representation Unchanged

Huddersfield

SIR J. T. WOODHOUSE (R)

1895—Sir J. T. Woodhouse (R) 6755
    Sir J. Crosland (C).. 5868
    H. R. Smart (Lab).. 1594

        Majority 887

1892 — Summers (R), 7098; Crosland (C), 6837:
Majority, 261. Bye-election (Feb. 1893)—
Crosland (C), 7058; Woodhead (R), 7033:
Majority, 35
        Radical Gain

SIR

1895—Sir H. S.
    F. Maddi

1892—King (C)
    Maddison

        Rep

Hull (West)
MR. C. H. WILSON (R)

1895—C. H. Wilson (R)	.. ..	6637
T. McCarthy (Lab)	.. ..	1400
	Majority	5237
1892—Wilson (R)	.. ..	6283
Smith (C)	.. ..	3500
	Majority	2783

Representation Unchanged

Hythe
GENERAL SIR B. EDWARDS (C)

1895—General Sir B. Edwards (C)	.. ..	2189
Sir J. Hart (R)	.. ..	1726
	Majority	463

1892—Sir E. Watkin, Bart. (LU) Unopposed

Representation Unchanged

Hull, East (See end of section)

MR. D. F.

| 1895—D. F. Godda |
| Sir C. Dalry |
| A. W. Soame |
| Lord Elcho (|

| | M |
| 1892— Dalrymple |
| Goddard (R |
| Majority, 29 |

Ipswich

SIR CHARLES DALRYMPLE (C)

1895—D. F. Goddard (R)	..	..	..	4396
Sir C. Dalrymple (C)	..	..	..	4293
A. W. Soames (R) ..	..	..	..	4250
Lord Elcho (C)	..	..	..	4219

Majority 43

1892—Dalrymple (C), 4350; Elcho (C), 4277; Goddard (R), 4054; Soames (R), 3888: Majority, 296

Radical Gain

Kidderminster

MR. A. F. GODSON, Q.C. (C)

1895—A. F. Godson (C) ..	..	..	..	2008
R. Eve (R) ..	..	..	..	1713

Majority 295

1892—Godson (C) ..	..	..	..	2066
Eve (R) ..	..	..	..	1801

Majority 265
Representation Unchanged

MR. T. G

1895—T. G. Bow	
H. Beaum	

1892—Bowles (C	
Kemp (R)	

Repr

Leeds (Central)	Leeds (East)	RT. HON

MR. GERALD W. BALFOUR (C)   **MR. T. R. LEUTY (R)**   RT. HON

1895—G. W. Balfour (C) 4631
        L. Jones (R) 3977

               Majority 654

1892—Balfour (C) 4448
        Walton (R) 4335

               Majority 113
       Representation Unchanged

1895—T. R. Leuty (R) 3856
        J. D. Power (C) 3145

             Majority 711

1892—Lawrence Gane (R), 4024; Morton (C), 3197;
      Majority, 827. Bye-Election (April, 1895)—
      Leuty (R), 3999; Power (C), 2868; Majority,
1131
       Representation Unchanged

1895—Rt Hon W
        H. S. Ba

1892—Jackson
        Leuty (R

            Rep

Leeds (South)	Leeds (West)	

MR. J. L. WALTON, Q.C. (R)

**RT. HON. HERBERT J. GLAD-
STONE (R)**

MR. HEN

1895—J. L. Walton (R) 4608
R. Neville (C) 4447
A. Shaw (Lab) 622

Majority 161

1892—Sir L. Playfair (R), 4829; Neville (C), 3294:
Majority, 1535. Bye-election (Sept., 1892)—
Walton (R), 4414; Neville (C), 3466:
Majority, 948

Representation Unchanged

1895—Rt Hon H. J. Gladstone (R) 6314
Colonel North (C) 6218

Majority 96

1892—Gladstone (R) 5974
Greenwood (C) 5621

Majority 353
Representation Unchanged

1895.—H. Bro:
W. Haz
J. F. R
J. Burg

1892—J. A. P
Returne
—Broad
Rollesto
Majorit
R

Leicester

MR. WALTER HAZELL (R)

1895—H. Broadhurst (R) 9792
      W. Hazell (R) 7753
      J. F. Rolleston (C) 7654
      J. Burgess (Lab) 4009

           Majority 99

1892—J. A. Picton (R) and Sir J. Whitehead (R),
      Returned Unopposed. Bye-election (1894)—
      Broadhurst (R), 9464; Hazell (R), 7184;
      Rolleston (C), 6967; Burgess (Lab), 4402:
      Majority, 217
        Representation Unchanged

Liverpool (Abercromby)

MR. W. F. LAWRENCE (C)

1895—Unopposed

1892—W. F. Lawrence (C) 3677
      Bowring (R) 2606

          Majority 1071
        Representation Unchanged

Lincoln (See end of section)

Live

RT. HON. F

1895 —Baron De
     C, T. Da

1892— De Worm
     Paul (R)

     Re

Liverpool (Everton)	**Liverpool (Exchange)**
MR. J. A. WILLOX (C)	MR. J. C. BIGHAM, Q.C. (C)

<table>
<tr><td>1895—Unopposed</td><td></td><td>1895—J. C. Bigham (C)</td><td>2884</td></tr>
<tr><td>1892—Willox (C)</td><td>3954</td><td>W. B. Bowring (R)</td><td>2630</td></tr>
<tr><td>Atkin (R)</td><td>2165</td><td></td><td></td></tr>
<tr><td></td><td></td><td>Majority</td><td>254</td></tr>
<tr><td>Majority</td><td>1789</td><td>1892—Neville (R)</td><td>2721</td></tr>
<tr><td>Representation Unchanged</td><td></td><td>Bigham (C)</td><td>2655</td></tr>
<tr><td></td><td></td><td>Majority</td><td>66</td></tr>
<tr><td></td><td></td><td>Conservative Gain</td><td></td></tr>
</table>

SIR G. S. F

1895—Sir G. :
B. S. J

1892—Baden-
Threlfa

R

Liverpool (Scotland)

MR. T. P. O'CONNOR (AP)

1895—T. P. O'Connor (AP)	..	..	..	..	2089
W. E. Macartney (C)	..	..	..	..	1452
Majority	..	..	..	..	637
1892—O'Connor (AP)..	..	..	..	..	2537
Vesey-Fitzgerald (C)	..	..	..	..	1432
Majority	..	..	..	..	1105

Representation Unchanged

Liverpool (Walton)

MR. J. HENRY STOCK (C)

1895—Unopposed					
1892—J. H. Stock (C)	..	..	..	..	3707
Dr. Richardson (R)	..	..	..	..	2493
Majority	..	..	..	1214

Representation Unchanged

Liverpool, West Toxteth (See end of section)

Liverpo

RT. HON. WA

1895—Rt Hon W. H			
Oscar Browni			
		Ma,	
1892—W. H. Cross			
Majority, 11			
1893)—Long			
Majority, 1357			
	Represer		

Maidstone

SIR F. SEAGER HUNT (C)

1895—Unopposed
1892—Cornwallis (C) 2443
    Nussey (R) 1627
             Majority 816
Representation Unchanged

Manchester (East)

THE RT. HON. A. J. BALFOUR (C)

1895—The Rt Hon A. J. Balfour (C) 5386
    Prof J. E. Munro (R) 4610
            Majority 776
1892—A. J. Balfour (C) 5147
    Munro (R).. 4749
            Majority 398
Representation Unchanged

M

MR. C.

1895—C. E. Sch
    A. H. Mo
1892—Schwann
    Yates (C)
        Rep

Manchester (North-East)

RT. HON. SIR JAS. FERGUSSON (C)

1895—The Rt Hon Sir J. Fergusson (C)	..		3961
E. Holt (R)	..	..	..	..	3720
J. Johnson (Lab)	..	..	..	..	546
Majority	..	..	..	241
1892—Fergusson (C) ..	..	..	..	..	4239
Scott (R)	..	..	..	..	4129
Majority	..	..	..	110

Representation Unchanged

Manchester (North-West)

SIR W. H. HOULDSWORTH (C)

1895—Sir W. H. Houldsworth (C)..	..	..	4997
T. F. Byrne (R)	..	..	..	3526
Majority	..	..	..	1471

1892—Houldsworth (C) Unopposed

Representation Unchanged

M

THE RT.

OF

1895—Rt Hon

Sir H. E

1892—Roscoe (

Emlyn (C

Manchester (South-West)

MR. W. J. GALLOWAY (C)

1895— W. J. Galloway (C)	3994
J. M. Astbury (R)	3496
Majority	498
1892—Jacob Bright (R)	3924
Professor Hopkinson (LU)	3776
Majority	148

Conservative Gain

Middlesborough

MR. J. H. WILSON (LAB)

1895—J. H. Wilson (Lab)..	6755
Colonel Sadler (C)	4735
Majority	2020
1892—Wilson (Lab)	4691
Robson (R)	4062
Bell (LU)	3333
Majority	629

Representation Unchanged

M

MR. A

1895—A. Spice	
E. M. U	
1892—Spicer (	
Elliott ((	
Re	

Morpeth

MR. THOMAS BURT (R)

1895—T. Burt (R)	.. ..	3404
M. Barry (C)	.. ..	1235
	Majority	2169

1892—T. Burt, Unopposed

Representation Unchanged

Newcastle-on-Tyne

MR. CHARLES F. HAMOND (C)

1895—C. F. Hamond (C)	.. ..	12833
W. D. Cruddas (C)	.. ..	12170
Rt Hon J. Morley (R)	.. .. ..	11862
J. Craig (R)	.. ..	11154
F. Hammill (Lab)	.. ..	2302

| Majority   .. .. | 971 |

1892—Hamond (C), 13823; Morley (R), 10905;
Craig (R), 10686: Majority, 2918. Bye-
Election (August. 1892)—Morley (R), 12983;
Ralli (LU), 11244: Majority, 1739
Conservative Gain

New

MR. W.

| 1895—C. F. Ham |
| W. D. Cru |
| Rt Hon J. |
| J. Craig (R |
| F. Hammill |

1892—Hamond
Craig (R),
Election (
Ralli (LU

Newcastle-under-Lyme
MR. W. S. ALLEN (R)

1895—W. S. Allen (R)	3510
A. M. Lee (LU)	3399
Majority	111
1892—Allen (R)	4204
Coghill (LU)	2936
Majority	1268

Representation Unchanged

Northampton
MR. HENRY LABOUCHERE (R)

1895—H. Labouchere (R)..	4884
G. C. A. Drucker (C)	3820
E. Harford (R)	3703
J. Jacobs (C)	3394
W. Jones (Soc).. .. :	1216
J. M. Robertson (IR)	1131
Majority	1064

1892—Labouchere (R), 5436; Manfield (R), 5161;
Richards (C), 3651; Drucker (C), 3235;
Majority, 1785

Conservative Gain of One

MR. G

1895—H. Lab
G. C. A
E. Har
J. Jacc
W. Jon
J. M. ?

1892—Labou
Richar
Majori
C

Norwich

MR. SAMUEL HOARE (C)

1895—S. Hoare (C)	..	..	..	..	..	..	8166
Sir H. Bullard (C)	..	..	..	..	..	8034
T. Terrell (R)	..	..	..	..	..	7330
F. W. Verney (R)	..	..	..	..	..	7210

Majority 836

1892—Hoare (C), 7718; Colman (R), 7407; Bedford (R), 6811: Majority, 311
Conservative Gain of One

Norwich

SIR. H. BULLARD (C)

1895—S. Hoare (C)	..	..	..	..	..	..	8166
Sir H. Bullard (C)	..	..	..	..	..	8034
T. Terrell (R)	..	..	..	..	..	7330
F. W. Verney (R)	..	..	..	..	..	7210

Majority 704

1892—Hoare (C), 7718; Colman (R), 7407; Bedford (R), 6811: Majority, 311
Conservative Gain of One

N

MR

1895—E. Bond
Rt Hon

1892—Morley (
Finch-H

Nottingham (South)

LORD H. BENTINCK (C)

1895—Lord H. Bentinck (C)	.. ..	4802
F. W. Maude (R)	. .. .	4369
	Majority	433
1892—Wright (C)	.. ..	4570
Fletcher Moulton (R)	.. ..	4487
	Majority	83

Representation Unchanged

Nottingham (West)

MR. J. H. YOXALL (R)

1895—J. H. Yoxall (R)	.. ..	6088
A. G. Sparrow (LU)	.. ..	5575
	Majority	513
1892—Seely (LU)	.. ..	5610
Broadhurst (R)	.. ..	5309
	Majority	301

Radical Gain

MR. R

1895—R. Ascroft (		
J. F. Oswal		
A. Lee (R).		
Rt Hon Sir		

1892—Cheetham (
Elliott Lee
Majority, 4
Conse

Oldham

MR. J. F. OSWALD, Q.C. (C)

1895—R. Ascroft (C) 13085
J. F. Oswald (C) 12465
A. Lee (R).. 12294
Rt Hon Sir J. T. Hibbert (R) 12092

Majority 171

1892—Cheetham (R), 12619; Hibbert (R), 12541;
Elliott Lees (C), 12205; Maclean (C), 11952:
Majority, 336
Conservative Gain of Two

Oxford (City)

VISCOUNT VALENTIA (C)

1895—Viscount Valentia (C) 3623
T. H. Kingerlee (R) 2975

Majority 648

1892 — Chesney (C), 3276; Souttar (R), 3156:
Majority, 120. Bye-election (April, 1895)—
Lord Valentia (C), 3745; Little (R), 3143:
Majority, 602
Representation Unchanged

MR. RO

1895—R. Purvis
A. C. Mor

1892—Morton (R
Purvis (L

Plymouth

SIR EDWARD CLARKE, Q.C. (C)

1895—Sir Edward Clarke (C) 5575
   C. Harrison (R) 5482
   Hon. E. Hubbard (C) 5456
   S. F. Mendl (R) 5298

     Majority 93

1892—Clarke (C).. 5081
   Sir W. Pearce (C) 5081
   C. Harrison (R) 4921
   Lidgett (R) 4861

     Majority 160
    Radical Gain of One

Plymouth

MR. C. HARRISON (R)

1895—Sir E. Clarke (C) 5575
   C. Harrison (R) 5482
   Hon E. Hubbard (C) 5456
   S. F. Mendl (R) 5298

     Majority 26

1892—Clarke (C), 5081 ; Pearse (C), 5081 ; Harrison
  (R), 4921 ; Lidgett (R), 4861 : Majority, 160
    Radical Gain of One

MR. T

1895—T. W. N
   J. F. Ho

1892—Winn (C)
   40. Bye
   1228 ; Sh
   election (
   on petiti
   (C), 1159

     Re

Portsmouth

SIR J. BAKER (R)

1895—Sir J. Baker (R) 10451
W. O. Clough (R) 10255
A. C. Harmsworth (C) 9717
Rt Hon E. Ashley (C) 9567

Majority 734

1892—Baker (R), 9643; Clough (R), 9448; Willis
(C), 9135; Ashley (C), 9000: Majority, 508

Representation Unchanged

Portsmouth ‖

MR. W. O. CLOUGH (R)

1895—Sir J. Baker (R) 10451
W. O. Clough (R) 10255
A. C. Harmsworth (C) 9717
Rt Hon E. Ashley (LU) .. .. .. 9567·

Majority 688

1892—Baker (R), 9643; Clough (R), 9448; Willis
(C), 9135; Ashley (LU), 9000: Majority, 448

Representation Unchanged

RT. H
1895—Rt
W.
J. T

1892—Har
Tom
Wel

Preston

MR. W. E. M. TOMLINSON (C)

1895—Rt Hon R. W. Hanbury (C)		8028
W. E M. Tomlinson (C)		7622
J. Tattersall (Lab)		4781
Majority		2841
1892—Hanbury (C)		8070
Tomlinson (C)		7764
Weld-Blundell (R)		6182
Majority		1582
Representation Unchanged		

Reading

MR. C. T. MURDOCH (C)

1895—C. T. Murdoch (C)		4278
G. W. Palmer (R)		3927
Majority		351
1892—Palmer (R)		3900
Murdoch (C)		3700
Majority		200
Conservative Gain		

MR. C.

1895—C. M. Royds		
W. L. Bright		
G. Barnes (La		
Ma		
1892—Potter (L)		
Royds (C)		
Ma		
Cons		

Rochester

VISCOUNT CRANBORNE (C)

1895—Viscount Cranborne (C) 2152
C. Grenfell (R).. 1673

Majority 479

1892—Davies (C), 2119; Maddison (R), 1712:
Majority, 407. Bye-Election (February,
1893)—Lord Cranborne Returned Unopposed

Representation Unchanged

St. Helens

MR. H. SETON-KARR (C)

1895—H. S-Karr (C) 4700
J. Forster (R) 4091

Majority 609

1892—Seton-Karr (C).. 4258
Kennedy (R) 4199

Majority 59
Representation Unchanged

MR. F.

1895—F. Platt-H
W. H. Ho

1892—Holland (
Baumann

Salford (South)
SIR HENRY HOYLE HOWORTH (C)

1895—Sir H. H. Howorth (C)..	.. .. ..	3384
A. Forrest (R).. ..	..	3310
H. W. Hobart (Lab)	..	813
Majority	..	74
1892—Howorth (C)	..	3406
Forrest (R)	..	3369
Hall (Lab)..	..	553
Majority	.. ..	37
Representation Unchanged		

Salford (West)
MR. LEES KNOWLES (C)

1895—L. Knowles (C)	.. .. ..	4354
Armitage (R) ..	..	4254
Majority	..	100
1892—Knowles (C)	..	4152
Armitage (R) ..	..	4112
Majority	.. ..	40
Representation Unchanged		

MR.

1895—E. H. H
W. R. B

1892—Hulse (C
Brown (

Re

Scarborough

MR. J. C. RICKETT (R)

1895—J. C. Rickett (R)	..	.. ..	2415
Sir G. R. Sitwell (C)	..	..	2391
	Majority	..	24
1892—Sitwell (C)..	.. .. ..	..	2293
Rowntree (R)	.. ..	..	2122
	Majority	.. .. ..	171
	Radical Gain		

Sheffield (Attercliffe)

MR. BATTY LANGLEY (R)

1895—Unopposed

1892—Hon B. Coleridge (R), 5107; Smith (C), 3963; Majority, 1144. Bye-Election, (July, 1894)—Langley (R), 4486; Hill-Smith (C), 3495; F. Smith (Lab), 1249; Majority, 991

Representation Unchanged

S

RT. HON

1895—Unopp

1892—Rt Hon
Deane

R

Sheffield (Central)

COLONEL HOWARD VINCENT (C)

1895—Unopposed

1892—Colonel Howard Vincent (C)	..	..	**4474**
Cameron (R)	.. .. ..		**3618**
Majority	.. .. ..	..	**856**

Representation Unchanged

Sheffield (Eccleshall)

SIR E. ASHMEAD BARTLETT (C)

1895—Unopposed

1892—Sir E. Ashmead Bartlett (C)	..	..	**4536**
Leader (R)..	.. .. ..	.	**3696**
Majority	.. .. ..	..	**840**

Representation Unchanged

MR. C. I

1895—Unop

1892—C. B.
Hamr

Shrewsbury

MR. H. D. GREENE, Q.C. (C)

1895—Unopposed

1892—Greene 1979
    Batten 1573

            Majority 406

    Representation Unchanged

Southampton

SIR J. B. SIMEON (C)

1895—T. Chamberlayne (C) 5955
    Sir J. B. Simeon (C) 5413
    Sir F. H. Evans (R) 5167
    H. G. Wilson (R) 4159
    Macdonald (Lab) 866

          Majority 246

1892—Chamberlayne (C), 5449; Evans (R), 5182;
    Burt (R), 4920; Giles (C), 4734: Majority,
    448
        Conservative Gain of One

MR. T. C

1895—T. Chambe
    Sir J. Sime
    Sir F. H.
    H. G. Wil
    Macdonald

1892—Chamberla
    Burt (R),
    267
        Con

South Shields		Stafford		S
MR. W. S. ROBSON, Q.C. (R)		**MR. C. E. SHAW (R)**		**MR. T. H.**

1895—W. S. Robson (R) 5057
      H. H. Wainwright (C) 4924

          Majority   133

1892—Stevenson (R) 4965
      Wainwright (C) 3958

          Majority   1007
    Representation Unchanged

1895—C. E. Shaw (R)   1568
      T. Salt (C)   1556

          Majority   12

1892—Shaw (R) 1684
      Straight (C)   1322

          Majority   362
    Representation Unchanged

1895—T. H. Sidebo
      G. M. Wrigh

          M

1892—Sidebottom (
      Wright (R)

          M
    Represe

Stockport

MR. G. WHITELEY (C)

1895—G. Whiteley (C)	5410
B. V. Melville (C)	5067
Sir J. Leigh (R)	4933
J. Roskill (R)	4562
Majority	477

1892—Leigh (R), 5202; L. Jennings (C), 4986; Major Hume (R), 4876; Hon P. Bowes Lyon (C), 4681: Majority, 110. Bye-election (1893) —Whiteley (C), 5264; Major Hume (R), 4799: Majority, 465

    Conservative Gain of One

Stockport

MR. B. V. MELVILLE (C)

1895—G. Whiteley (C)	5410
B. V. Melville (C)	5067
Sir J. Leigh (R)	4933
J. Roskill (R)	4562
Majority	134

1892—Leigh (R), 5202; Jennings (C), 4986; Hume (R), 4876; Bowes Lyon (C), 4681: Majority, 195. Bye-election (Feb., 1893)—Whiteley (C), 5264; Sharp-Hume (R), 4799: Majority, 465

    Conservative Gain of One

S

MR.

1895—J. Samuel	
T. Wrigh	

1892—Wrightson
Davey (R)

Stoke-on-Trent
MR. D. H. COGHILL (LU)

1895—D. H. Coghill (LU)   4396
      G. G. Leveson-Gower (R)   4196

        Majority   200

1892—Leveson-Gower (R)   4629
      Walters (C)   2846

        Majority   .. . • ..   1783
        Liberal Unionist Gain

Sunderland
MR. W. T. DOXFORD (C)

1895—W. T. Doxford (C)..   9833
      Sir E. T. Gourley (R)   8232
      Samuel Storey (R)   8185

        Majority   1601

1892—Storey (R), 9711; Gourley (R), 9554; Lamb-
    ton (LU), 8394; Pemberton (C), 8002;
    Majority, 1317
        Conservative Gain of One

SIR E.

1895—W. T. D{
      Sir E. T.
      S. Storey

1892—Storey (R
    ton (LU
    Majority,
        Co

Taunton
LIEUT-COL. WELBY (C)

1895—Unopposed

1892—Allsopp (C) 1402
  Bridgman (R) 921
           ——
    Majority 481
  Representation Unchanged

Tynemouth
MR. R. S. DONKIN (C)

1895—R. S. Donkin (C) 3168
  F. D. Blake (R) 2959
           ——
    Majority 209

1892—Donkin (C) 3121
  Annand (R) 2783
           ——
    Majority 338
  Representation Unchanged

VISCOU

1895—Lord Milt
  H. S. L.

1892—Charleswo
  Strachan (

  Repr

Walsall

MR. S. GEDGE (C)

| 1895—S. Gedge (C) | .. | .. | .. | 5145 |
| Sir A. D. Hayter (R) | .. | .. | .. | 4828 |

Majority 317

1892—James (C), 5226; Holden (R), 4909: Majority,
317. Bye-election (February, 1893)—Hayter
(R), 5235; Ritchie (C), 5156: Majority, 79

Conservative Gain

Warrington

MR. R. PIERPOINT (C)

| 1895—R. Pierpoint (C) | .. | .. | .. | 4001 |
| P. B. Scott (R) | .. | .. | .. | 3326 |

Majority 675

| 1892—Pierpoint (C) | .. | .. | .. | 3843 |
| Houston (R) | .. | .. | .. | 3258 |

Majority 585
Representation Unchanged

Warw[ick]

THE HON.

1895—Unopposed

1892—Rt Hon A
opposed.
Lyttelton (
Majority, 9

Repr[esentation]

Wednesbury	West Bromwich	MR.

Wednesbury
MR. W. D. GREEN (C)

1895—W. D. Green (C) 4924
    C. Roberts (R) . 4733

        Majority . 191

1892—Lloyd (C) 4986
    Stanhope (R) 4926

        Majority 60
        Representation Unchanged

West Bromwich
MR. J. ERNEST SPENCER (C)

1895—Unopposed
1892—Spencer (C) 4474
    Roberts (R) 3429

        Majority 1045
        Representation Unchanged

MR. .

1895—A. Helder
    T. S. Litt

1892—Little (R)
    Bain (C)

Wigan

SIR F. S. POWELL (C)

1895—Sir F. S. Powell (C)	..	..	..	..	3949
T. Aspinwall (Lab)	..	..	..	..	3075

Majority 874

1892—Powell (C)	..	..	..	..	3422
Aspinwall (Lab)	..	..	..	..	3312

Ma'ority 110
Representation Unchanged

Winchester

MR. W. H. MYERS (C)

1895—Unopposed

1892—W. H. Myers (C) ..	..	..	..	..	1213
C. W. Mathews (R)	.:	.:	..	..	859

Majority 354
Representation Unchanged

MR. I

Repi

Wolverhampton (East)

RT. HON. SIR H. H. FOWLER (R)

1895—Rt Hon Sir H. H. Fowler (R) 4011
R. E. Kettle (C) 2977

Majority 1034

1892—H. H. Fowler Unopposed

Representation Unchanged

Wolverhampton (South)

THE RT. HON. C. P. VILLIERS (LU)

1895—Unopposed

1892—Unopposed

Representation Unchanged

Wol

SIR ALF

1895—Sir Alfred
G. R. Th

1892—Hickman
Plowden

Rep

Worcester	Yarmouth (Great)	
HON. G. H. ALLSOPP (C)	**CAPTAIN SIR J. C. COLOMB (C)**	**MR. J.**

Worcester

HON. G. H. ALLSOPP (C)

1895—Hon G. H. Allsopp (C)	3530
T. Hinks (R)	2328
Majority	1202
1892—Allsopp (C)	3353
Howard (R)	2540
Majority	813

Representation Unchanged

Yarmouth (Great)

CAPTAIN SIR J. C. COLOMB (C)

1895—Captain J. C. Colomb (C)	3528
J. M. Moorsom, Q.C. (R)	2893
Majority	635
1892—Moorsom (R)	2972
Tyler (C)	2704
Majority	268

Conservative Gain

MR. J.

1895—J. G. Butc	
Sir F. Loc	
A. E. Pea:	
1892—Butcher (C	
Lockwood	
Pease (R)	

Repr

York City
SIR FRANK LOCKWOOD, Q.C. (R)

1895—	J. G. Butcher (C)	5516
	Sir F. Lockwood (R)	5309
	A. E. Pease (R)	5214
	Majority	207
1892—	Butcher (C)	5076
	Lockwood (R)	5030
	Pease (R)	4846
	Majority	46

Representation Unchanged

Devonport
MR. E. J. C. MORTON (R)

1895—	i. E. Kearley (R)	3570
	E. J. C. Morton (R)	3511
	P. Wippell (LU)	3303
	Captain T. Thynne (C)..	3263
	Majority	208
1892—	Kearley (R)	3354
	Morton (R)	3325
	Price (C)	3012
	Harvey (C)	2972
	Majority	313

Representation Unchanged

MR. C

1895—	C. H. See	
	W. Crosfi	
1892—	Crosfield	
	Kerans (C	

L

Hull (East)
MR. T. FIRBANK (C)

1895—	T. Firbank (C)..	4302
	Sir C. Smith (R)	4152
	Majority	150
1892—	Smith (R)	4570
	Grotrian (C)	3738
	Majority	832

Conservative Gain

Live
MR. R

1895—	R. P. He	
	W. Mulh	
1822—	Houston	
	Griffith (I	

Rep

Bedfordshire (Luton)

MR. T. G. ASHTON (R)

1895—T. G. Ashton (R) **5430**
Colonel O. T. Duke (LU) **5244**

Majority 186

1892—Flower (R), 5296; Duke (LU), 4277:
Majority, 1019. Bye-election (Sept., 1892—
Mr. Flower raised to the peerage)—Whit-
bread (R), 4838; Duke (LU), 4596: Majority,
242

Representation Unchanged

|Berkshire (Abingdon)

MR. A. K. LOYD, Q.C. (C)

1895—A. K. Loyd (C) **4064**
C. A. Pryce (R) **3019**

Majority 1045

1892—Wroughton (C) **3565**
Pryce (R) **3239**

Majority 326
Representation Unchanged

Bedfordshire, Biggleswade (See end of section)

Ber

MR. W.

1895—W. G. Moun
Sir J. Swinbr

M

1892—Mount (C)..
Stevens (R)

M
Represe

Berkshire (Wokingham)

SIR GEORGE RUSSELL, BART. (C)

1895—Unopposed
1892—Sir G. Russell (C) 4986
F. J. Patton (R) 2738

Majority 2248
Representation Unchanged

Bucks (Aylesbury)

BARON F. DE ROTHSCHILD (LU)

1895—Unopposed
1892—Baron F. de Rothschild (LU) 5515
T. H. Dolbey (R) 2002

Majority 2523
Representation Unchanged

MR.

1895—W. W.
H. S. L

1892—Leon (R
Carlile

Bucks (Wycombe)

VICOUNT CURZON (C)

95 —Unopposed
92—Lord Curzon (C) 5030
    A. Hope Hawkins (R) . . . 3988

    Majority 1042
Representation Unchanged

Cambridgeshire (Chesterton)

MR. R. GREENE (C)

1895—R. Greene (C) 4432
    H. E. Hoare (R) . . . 4012

    Majority . . 420
1892—Hoare (R) 4350
    Hall (C) 3952

    Majority . . . 398
    Conservative Gain

Camb

MR. F

1895—H. McC
    Sir G. N

1892—Newnes
    Giffard

Cambridgeshire (Wisbech)

MR. C. T. GILES (C)

1895—C. T. Giles (C).. 4368
Hon A. G. Brand (R) 4145

Majority 223

1892—Brand (R), 4311; Duncan (C), 4189:
Majority, 122. Bye-Election (April, 1894)—
Brand (R), 4368; Sackville (C), 4227:
Majority, 136
Conservative Gain

Cheshire (Altrincham)

MR. CONINGSBY DISRAELI (C)

1895—C. R. Disraeli (C) 5264
A. M. Latham (R).. 3889

Majority 1375

1892—Disraeli (C) 5056
Leadam (R) 4258

Majority 798
Representation Unchanged

HO.

1895—Hon R
W. S.

1892—Maclar
Chatte

Cheshire (Eddisbury)

MR. H. J. TOLLEMACHE (C)

1895—H. J. Tollemache (C)		5176
R. Bate (R)		3371
	Majority	1805
1892—Tollemache (C)..		4578
Tomlinson (R)..		4042
Majority		536

Representation Unchanged

Cheshire (Hyde)

MR. J. W. SIDEBOTHAM (C)

1895—J. W. Sidebotham (C)		4735
G. W. Rhodes (R)		3844
G. S. Christie (Lab)		448
	Majority	891
1892—Sidebotham (C)		4525
Ashton (R)		4220
Majority		305

Representation Unchanged

HON. A.

1895—Unop

1892—Hon .
    A. M

Cheshire (Macclesfield)

MR. W. BROMLEY-DAVENPORT (C)

1895—Unopposed

1892—W. Bromley-Davenport (C)	.. ..	4332
J. C. McCoan (R)	.. .	3396
	Majority	936

Representation Unchanged

Cheshire (Northwich)

SIR J. T. BRUNNER, BART. (R)

1895—Sir J. T. Brunner (R)	.. .. ..	5706
T. Ward (C)	.. .. . .	4068
	Majority	1638
1892—Brunner (R)	.. ..	5580
Whiteley (C)	.. ..	4325
	Majority	1255

Representation Unchanged

Che

COL. E. T. D. C

1895—Unopposed

1892—Colonel Co
    B. C. De L

M

Repres

Cornwall (Bodmin)

RT. HON. LEONARD H. COURTNEY (LU)

1895—Rt Hon L. H. Courtney (LU) 4035
J. McDougall (R) 3492

Majority 543

1892—Courtney (LU) 3809
McDougall (R) 3578

Majority 231
Representation Unchanged

Cornwall (Camborne)

MR. A. STRAUSS (LU)

1895—A. Strauss (LU) 3166
C. A. V. Conybeare (R) 2704

Majority 462

1892—Conybeare (R) 3073
Strauss (LU) 2635

Majority 438
Liberal Unionist Gain

MR.

1895—T. Ow
F. Wi

1892—Owen
Moles

Cornwall (St. Austell)

MR. W. McARTHUR (R)

1895—W. McArthur (R)	..	..	..	4192
W. Williams (LU)	..	..	..	3092
	Majority	..	..	1101
1892—McArthur (R)	..	..	..	4201
Westlake (LU)	..	..	..	2593
	Majority	..	..	1608

Representation Unchanged

Cornwall (St. Ives)

MR. T. B. BOLITHO (LU)

1895—Unopposed

1892—Unopposed

Representation Unchanged

C

MR. E.

1895—E. Lawren
H. T. Wa

1892—Williams
Lile (R)

Rep

Cumberland (Cockermouth)

SIR WILFRID LAWSON, BT. (R)

1895—Sir W. Lawson (R)	.. ..		4259
T. Milvain, Q.C. (C)	.. ..		4018
	Majority	.. .. ..	241
1892—Lawson (R)	.. .. ..		4599
Scott Napier (C)	.. ..		3828
	Majority	.. .. ..	71
	Representation Unchanged		

Cumberland (Egremont)

HON H. V. DUNCOMBE (C)

1895—Hon H. V. Duncombe (C)	.. .. ..		3717
D. Ainsworth (R)	.. .. ..		3586
	Majority	.. .. ..	131
1892—Ainsworth (R)	.. .. ..		3849
Lord Muncaster (C)	.. .. ..		3378
	Majority	.. .. ..	471
	Conservative Gain		

Cu

MR. R

1895—R. A. All		
H. C. H		
1892—Allison (I		
Howard		
	Re	

Cumberland (Penrith)

MR. J. W. LOWTHER (C)

1895—J. W. Lowther (C)	.. ..	3868
Dr. T. S. Douglas (R)	.. ..	3268
Majority	.. .. ..	600
1892—Lowther (C)	.. ..	3549
Douglas (R)	.. ..	3424
Majority	.. .. ..	125

Representation Unchanged

Derbyshire (Chesterfield)

MR. T. BAYLEY (R)

1895—T. Bayley (R)	.. ..	4572
A. W. Byron (C)	.. ..	4325
Majority	.. .. ..	247
1892—Bayley (R)	.. ..	4249
Barnes (LU)	.. ..	4069
Majority	.. .. ..	180

Representation Unchanged

De

COLONEL

1895—Colonel	
A. G. S	
1892—Sidebo	
Cheeth	

R

Derbyshire (Ilkeston)

SIR BALTHAZAR FOSTER (R)

1895—Sir B. W. Foster (R)	6215	
Captain Baumgarten (C)	5254	
Majority	961	
1892—Foster (R)	6185	
Leeke (C)	4402	
Majority	1783	
Representation Unchanged		

Derbyshire (Mid)

MR. J. A. JACOBY (R)

1895—J. A. Jacoby (R)	4926	
W. C. Bridgman (C)	4351	
Majority	575	
1892—Jacoby (R)	4899	
Sanders (C)	3907	
Majority	992	
Representation Unchanged		

De

MR. J.

1895—J. A. Gret
H. E. Bro

1892—Broad (R)

Derbyshire, M

Derbyshire (West)

HON. VICTOR CAVENDISH (LU)

1895—Unopposed
1892—Hon V. Cavendish (LU) 5961
 The McDermott (R) 2768
 ───
 Majority 3193
 Representation Unchanged

Devonshire (Ashburton)

RT. HON. C. SEALE HAYNE (R)

1895—Rt Hon C. Seale Hayne (R) 4380
 J. A. Nix (C) 3970
 ───
 Majority 410
1892—Seale Hayne (R) 4361
 Collins (C).. 3649
 ───
 Majority 712
 Representation Unchanged

Dev

SIR W. CA

1895—Sir W.
 A. Bills
1892—Billson
 White (

Devonshire (Honiton)

SIR JOHN KENNAWAY, BART. (C)

1895—Unopposed

1892—Sir J. Kennaway (C) 4591
    Dr. Aubrey (R) 2565

    Majority 2026
    Representation Unchanged

Devonshire (South Molton)

MR. G. LAMBERT (R)

1895—G. Lambert (R) 4283
    Professor Long (LU) 2923

    Majority 1360

1892—Lambert (R) 4278
    More-Stevens (C) 2939

    Majority 1339
    Representation Unchanged

Dev

MR. H.

1895—H. F. Lu
    Colonel \

1892—Luttrell
    W-Thoṛ

R

Devonshire (Tiverton)

COL. SIR W. H. WALROND, BT. (C)

1895—Unopposed

1892—Sir W. H. Walrond (C).. 4433
Sir J. B. Phear (R) 3110

Majority 1323
Representation Unchanged

Devonshire (Torquay)

COM. A. S. PHILLPOTTS (C)

1895—Commander A. S. Phillpotts (C).. .. 4205
F. L. Barrett (R) 4030

Majority 175
1892—Mallock (C) 4157
Hayter (R) 3763

Majority 394
Representation Unchanged

De

MR. F.

1895—F. B. Mil
A. J. Spa

1892—Mildmay
Lush (R)

Rep

Dorsetshire (East)	Dorsetshire (North)	Dors

THE HON. H. STURT (C) MR. J. K. WINGFIELD-DIGBY (C) MR. W. I

1895—Unopposed

1892—Unopposed

Representation Unchanged

1895—Unopposed

1892—J. K. W-Digby (C) 3981
A. Arnold (R) 3456

Majority 525

Representation Unchanged

1895—Unopposed

1892—W. E. Bryme
E. Pearce-Ed

Ma

Represei

Dorsetshire (West)

COL. R. WILLIAMS (C)

1895—Unopposed

1892—Farquharson (C), 3691; Gatty (R), 2813:
Majority, 878. Bye-election (May, 1895)—
Williams (C), 3538; Homes (Lab), 2325:
Majority, 1213

Representation Unchanged

Durham (Barnard Castle)

SIR J. W. PEASE (R)

1895—Sir J. W. Pease (R)	4924
Captain W. L. Vane (LU)	3848
Majority	1076
1892—Pease (R)	5337
Rolley (C)	2924
Majority	2413
Representation Unchanged	

Dur

MR.

1895—J. M.
G. E.

1892—Paulton
Waddin

R

Durham (Chester-le-Street)

SIR JAMES JOICEY, BART. (R)

1895—Sir J. Joicey (R)	7370
Viscount Morpeth (LU)	4113
Majority	3257
1892—Joicey (R)	6453
Sullivan (LU)	4066
Majority	2387

Representation Unchanged

Durham County (Jarrow)

SIR C. M. PALMER (R)

1895—Unopposed

1892—Sir C. M. Palmer (R)	7343
E. D. Lewis (Lab)	2416
Majority	4927

Representation Unchanged

Durham

MR. A. F

1895—A. R. Came	
V. W. Corb	
M	
1892—Fenwick (R	
Wood (C) ..	
Hargrove (T	
M	

Repres

Durham (Mid)
MR. J. WILSON (R)

1895—J. Wilson (R)	5937
A. Wilkinson (C)	4295
Majority	1642
1892—Wilson (R)	5661
Hunter (C)	3699
Majority	1962
Representation Unchanged	

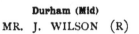

Durham (North-West)
MR. L. ATHERLY JONES (R)

1895—L. Atherley Jones (R)	5428
J. Joicey (C)	3869
Majority	1559
1892—Atherley Jones (R)..	5121
Dunville (LU)	2891
Majority	2230
Representation Unchanged	

Dur
SIR H. HA

1895—Sir H. Hav	
J. Richards	
1892—Richardson	
Havelock·A	
Lib	

Essex (Chelmsford)

MR. T. USBORNE (C)

1895—Unopposed

1892—T. Usborne (C)	.. ..	4168
Dr. Grigsby (R)	.. ..	2779
Majority	.. ..	1389

Representation Unchanged

Essex (Epping)

LIEUT-COL. MARK LOCKWOOD (C)

1895—Unopposed

1892—Lt.-Colonel Lockwood (C)	.. .. ..	4486
S. B. Heward (R)	.. ..	2738
Majority	.. .. ..	1748

Representation Unchanged

E

MR.

1895—J. Round (
R. Varty (

1892—Round (C)
Varty (R)

Repr

Essex, Maldon (See end of section)

Essex (Saffron Walden)

MR. C. GOLD (R)

1895—C. Gold (R)	..	..	..	..	..	..	3806
C. W. Gray (C)	..	..	..	..	..	..	3081
	Majority	..	..	..	..		725
1892—Gardner (R)	..	..	..	..	..	..	4564
Smith (C)	..	..	..	..	..	..	2683
	Majority	..	..	..	..		1881
	Representation Unchanged						

Essex (South-East)

MAJOR F. C. RASCH (C)

1895—Major Rasch (C)	..	..	..	..		5460
D. M. Watson (R)	..	..	..	..		3520
	Majority	..	..	..		1940
1892—Rasch (C)	..	..	..	..	..	4901
Brooks (R)	..	..	..	..	..	4359
	Majority	..	..	..		542
	Representation Unchanged					

Essex, Romford (See end of section)

E

MR. E

1895—E. W.			
A. H.			
1892—Byrne			
Whitti			

R

Gloucestershire (Cirencester)

HON. B. BATHURST (C)

1895—Hon B. Bathurst (C) 4509
     H. W. L. Lawson (R) 4294

           Majority 215

1892—Winterbottom (R), 4207; Chester-Master (C),
    4054: Majority, 153. Bye-Election (October,
    1892)—Chester-Master (C), 4277; Lawson (R),
    4274: Majority, 3. Bye-Election (February,
    1893—after Petition and a Tie Declared) —
    Lawson (R), 4687; Chester-Master (C), 4445:
    Majority, 242
          Conservative Gain

Gloucestershire (Forest of Dean)

RT. HON. SIR CHAS. DILKE (R)

1895—Unopposed

1892—Rt Hon Sir C. Dilke (R) 5360
     M. Colchester-Wemyss (C) 2942

          Majority 2418
      Representation Unchanged

Glou

MR. C.

1895—C. A. Crip
     C. P. Alle

1892—Brynmor
     Holloway

Gloucestershire (Tewkesbury)

SIR JOHN DORINGTON, BART. (C)

1895—Unopposed		
1892—Sir J. Dorington (C)	5028
Samuelson (R)..	4125
Majority	903
Representation Unchanged	

Gloucestershire (Thornbury)

MR. C. E. COLSTON (C)

1895—C. E. Colston (C)	5727
A. A. Allen (R)	4638
Majority	1089
1892—Colston (C)	5202
Howard (R)	4978
Majority	224
Representation Unchanged	

Ha

MR. W.

x

x

Repre

Hants (Basingstoke)	**Hants (Fareham)**	**Han**
MR. A. F. JEFFREYS (C)	LIEUT-GEN. SIR F. W. FITZ-WYGRAM, BART. (C)	SIR R. E

Hants (Basingstoke)

MR. A. F. JEFFREYS (C)

1895—Unopposed
1892—A. F. Jeffreys (C) 4064
    G. Judd (R) 2555

    Majority 1509
Representation Unchanged

Hants (Fareham)

LIEUT-GEN. SIR F. W. FITZ-WYGRAM, BART. (C)

1895—Unopposed
1892—General Sir F. W. FitzWygram (C) .. 6086
    J. G. Niven (R) 4547

    Majority 1539
Representation Unchanged

Han

SIR R. E

1895—Sir R. E.
    Hon A. W

1892—Webster (
    Mendl (R

    Repr

Hants (New Forest)

HON. J. SCOTT-MONTAGU (C)

1895—Unopposed

1892—Hon J. Scott-Montagu (C) 4481
    Joseph King (R) 3726

      Majority 755
  Representation Unchanged

Hants (Petersfield)

MR. W. WICKHAM (C)

1895—Unopposed

1892—W. Wickham (C) 3912
    Bonham-Carter (R) 3008

      Majority 904
  Representation Unchanged

Heref

MR.

1895—Unoppose

1892—J. Rankin
    J. Southa

    Rep

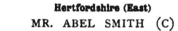

Herefordshire (Ross)

MR. M. BIDDULPH (LU)

1895—M. Biddulph (LU)	4573
A. Withey (R)	2828
Majority	1745
1892—Biddulph (LU)	4326
Pulley (R)	3869
Majority	457
Representation Unchanged	

Hertfordshire (East)

MR. ABEL SMITH (C)

1895—Unopposed

1892—A. Smith (C)	4276
E. R. Speirs (R)	2818
Majority	1458

Representation Unchanged

Her

MR. (

1895—Unoppos

1892—Hudson
Wattridg

Re

Hertfordshire (St. Albans)

MR. VICARY GIBBS (C)

1895—Unopposed

1892—Vicary Gibbs (C)	.. ..	3417
Harvey (R)	.. ..	2573
Bingham-Cox (C)	.. ..	1570

| Majority | .. .. .. | 844 |

Representation Unchanged

Hertfordshire (Watford)

MR. T. F. HALSEY (C)

1895—Unopposed

| 1892—T. F. Halsey (C) | .. .. | 4802 |
| J. Marnham (R) | .. .. | 3627 |

| Majority | .. .. .. | 1175 |

Representation Unchanged

Huntin

MR. A. H

1895—A. H. Sm
J. J. Wil

1892—Smith-Ba
Whitbrea

Rep

Huntingdonshire (Ramsey)	Kent (Ashford)	Ke
HON. ALWYN FELLOWES (C)	MR. L. HARDY (C)	RT. HON. SII

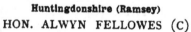

Huntingdonshire (Ramsey)

HON. ALWYN FELLOWES (C)

1895—Hon A. Fellowes (C)	..	..	..	..	3012
H. Heldmann (R) ..	..	..	..	..	2063
Majority	..	..	..	..	949
1892—Fellowes (C) ..	..	..	..	..	2842
Sheldon (R) ..	..	..	..	..	2445
Majority	..	..	..	..	397

Representation Unchanged

Kent (Ashford)

MR. L. HARDY (C)

1895—Unopposed

1892—L. Hardy (C) ..	..	..	..	..	5512
Bugler (R) ..	..	..	..	..	4281
Majority	..	..	..	..	1231

Representation Unchanged

Ke

RT. HON. SII

1895—Sir W. Hart		
Sir P. Nick		
M		
1892—Hart Dyke (		
Lyon (R) ..		
M		

Repres

Kent (Faversham)	Kent (Isle of Thanet)	
MR. F. G. BARNES (C)	RT. HON. JAMES LOWTHER (C)	MAJ

Kent (Faversham)

MR. F. G. BARNES (C)

1895—F. G. Barnes (C) 5738
S. Barrow (R) 4557

Majority 1181

1892—Knatchbull-Hugessen (C) 4844
Hallifax (R) 4640

Majority 204
Representation Unchanged

Kent (Isle of Thanet)

RT. HON. JAMES LOWTHER (C}

1895—Unopposed

1892—Rt Hon J. Lowther (C).. 3901
Heber Hart (R) 2857

Majority 1044
Representation Unchanged

MAJ

1895—Unop

1892—Majo
W. S

Kent (St. Augustine's)

RT. HON. A. AKERS-DOUGLAS (C)

1895—Unopposed
1892—Unopposed

Representation Unchanged

Kent (Sevenoaks)

MR. H. W. FORSTER (C)

1895—Unopposed
1892—Forster (C) 6036
    Johnston (R) 3908
                                    ————
            Majority 2128
        Representation Unchanged

Ken

MR. A. S. GRIF

1895—Unopposed
1892—A. S. G. Bos
    Captain Pav

            M;
        Represe

Lancashire (Accrington)

SIR F. J. LEESE, Q.C. (R)

1895—Sir F. J. Leese (R) 6168
W. Mitchell (C) 5828

Majority 340

1892—Leese (R), 6019; Hodge (C), 5472: Majority
547. Bye-election (Dec., 1893)—Leese, (R),
5822; Hodge (C), 5564: Majority, 258

Representation Unchanged

Lancashire (Blackpool)

SIR M. WHITE RIDLEY (C)

1895—Unopposed

1892—Sir M. White Ridley (C) 6536
Walker (R) 3487

Majority 3049

Representation Unchanged

Lancashire, Chorley (See end of section)

L

LIEUT-CO

1895—Unoppose

1892—Colonel S
A. Macd

Rep

Lancashire (Clitheroe)	Lancashire (Darwen)	Lan

SIR U. KAY-SHUTTLEWORTH (R)   **MR. J. RUTHERFORD (C)**   MR. O. I

1895—Unopposed

1892—Sir U. Kay-Shuttleworth (R) 7657
     W. E. Briggs (LU) 5506

     Majority 2151
     Representation Unchanged

1895—J. Rutherford (C) 7058
     C. P. Huntington (R) 6217

     Majority 841

1892—Huntington (R) 6637
     Viscount Cranborne (C) 6463

     Majority 174
     Conservative Gain

1895—O. L. Clare
     H. J. Roby

              N

1892—Roby (R) .
     Clare (C) .

              N
              C

Lancashire (Gorton)

MR. E. G. HATCH (C)

1895—E. G. Hatch (C)	..	..	..	..	..	5865
Dr. Pankhurst (R and Lab)	..	..	..	..	4261
Majority	..	..	..	..	1604
1892—Mather (R)	..	..	..	..	..	5255
Hatch (C)	..	..	..	..	..	5033
Majority	..	..	..	..	222
Conservative Gain						

Lancashire (Heywood)

MR. G. KEMP (LU)

1895—G. Kemp (LU)	..	..	..	..	..	4489
T. Snape (R)	..	..	..	..	..	3933
Majority	..	..	..	..	556
1892—Snape (R)	..	..	..	..	..	4366
Lawrence (LU)	..	..	..	..	3745
Majority	..	..	..	..	621
Liberal Unionist Gain						

COL.

1895—Colonel	
S. Wood	
1892—Woods	
Blunde	

Lancashire (Lancaster)
COLONEL FOSTER (C)

1895—Colonel Foster (C)	5028
L. S. Leadam (R)	4394
Majority	634
1892—Williamson (R)	4755
Storey (LU)	4075
Majority	680
Conservative Gain	

Lancashire (Leigh)
MR. C. P. SCOTT (R)

1895—C. P. Scott (R)	5130
W. A. Fitzgerald (C)	4453
Majority	677
1892—Wright (R)	4899
Jones (C)	3995
Majority	904
Representation Unchanged	

La
MR. R.

1895—R. Caven	
Baron Hi	
1892—Smith (R	
Crewdson	

L

Lancashire (Middleton)

MR. T. FIELDEN (C)

1895—T. Fielden (C) ..	..	..	..	..	..	5926
C. H. Hopwood, Q.C. (R)	..	..	..	..	5061
	Majority	..	..	..	..	865
1892—Hopwood (R) ..	..	..	..	..	..	5389
Fielden (C)	..	..	..	..	..	5273
	Majority	..	..	..	..	116
	Conservative Gain					

Lancashire (Newton)

HON. T. W. LEGH (C)

1895—Hon T. W. Legh (C)	..	..	..	..	5358
J. Moon (R) ..	..	..	..	..	..	3854
	Majority	..	..	..	..	1504
1892—Legh (C) ..	..	..	..	..	..	4713
Neil (R) ..	..	..	..	..	..	3819
	Majority	..	..	..	..	894
	Representation Unchanged					

Lan

RT. HON.

1895—Rt Hon		
J. Stoner		
1892—Forwood		
Middlehu		
	Rep	

Lancashire (Prestwich)

MR. F. CAWLEY (R)

1895—F. Cawley (R)	..	..	..	..	..	..	6039
R. G. Mowbray (C)		..	..	..	..	..	5938
	Majority		..	..	..	..	101
1892—Mowbray (C)	..	..	..	..	..	..	5718
Agnew (R)	..	..	..	..	..	..	5563
	Majority		..	..	..	..	155
	Radical Gain						

Lancashire (Radcliffe-cum-Farnworth)

COL. J. J. MELLOR (C)

1895—Colonel Mellor (C)	..	..	..	..	..	..	5525
Dr. Pollard (R)		..	..	..	..	..	4923
	Majority		..	..	..	..	602
1892—Leake (R)	..	..	..	..	..	..	4999
Mellor (C)	..	..	..	..	..	..	4904
	Majority		..	..	..	..	95
	Conservative Gain						

L

MR.

1895—Unop

1892—Made

Sparr

Lancashire (Southport)

RT. HON. G. N. CURZON (C)

1895—Rt Hon G. N. Curzon (C)	..	..	..	5163
Sir H. S. Naylor-Leyland (R)	..	..		4399
	Majority	..	..	..	764
1892—Curzon (C)..	..	..	..	..	4752
Dr. Pollard (R)	..	..	..		4148
	Majority	..	..	..	604
	Representation Unchanged				

Lancashire (Stretford)

MR. J. W. MACLURE (C)

1895—Unopposed					
1892—Maclure (C)	..	..	..	..	6623
Hall (R)	..	..	..	..	5278
	Majority	..	..	..	1345
	Representation Unchanged				

Lancashire, Westhoughton (See end of section)

Lan

MR. J.

1895—J. S. Gillia		
H. W. De		
1892—Gilliat (C)		
Deacon (R		
	Repr		

Leicestershire (Bosworth)

MR. C. B. McLAREN (R)

1895—C. B. McLaren (R)	..	..	..	..	5327
T. Cope (C)	..	..	..	..	..	4207
	Majority	..	..	..	..	1120
1892—McLaren (R)	..	..	..	..	..	5370
Hutton (C)	..	..	..	..	..	3846
	Majority	..	..	..	..	1524
Representation Unchanged					

Leicestershire (Harborough)

MR. J. W. LOGAN (R)

1895—J. W. Logan (R)	..	..	..	..	6699
Lieut Rowney (C)	..	..	..	..	5673
	Majority	..	..	..	..	1026
1892—Logan (R)	..	..	..	..	..	6244
Lowe (C)	..	..	..	..	..	5588
	Majority	..	..	..	..	656
Representation Unchanged					

L

LORD

1895—Lord E		
— Wal		
	N
1892—Marqui	
R	

Leicestershire

Lincolnshire (Brigg)	Lincolnshire (Gainsborough,	Linc
MR. H. J. RECKITT (R)	MR. E. BAINBRIDGE (R)	LD. WILL

Lincolnshire (Brigg)

1895—H. J. Reckitt (R) 4886
J. M. Richardson (C) 4110

Majority 776

1892—Waddy (R), 4448; Richardson (C), 4021:
Majority, 427. Bye-election (Dec. 1894)—
Richardson (C), 4377; Reckitt (R), 4300
Majority, 77
Radical Gain

Lincolnshire (Gainsborough,

1895—E. Bainbridge (R) 5077
E. Pearson (C).. 4301

Majority 776

1892—Bennett (R) 4945
Eyre (C) 4037

Majority 908
Representation Unchanged

Linc

LD. WILL

1895—Lord Wi
— Walla

1892—Stanhope
Majority
Willough
3744: M
Re

Lincolnshire (Louth)

MR. R. W. PERKS (R)

1895—R. W. Perks (R)		4191
Colonel F. A. Lucas (C)		3779
	Majority	412
1892—Perks (R)		4284
Heath (C)		3445
	Majority	839

Representation Unchanged

Lincolnshire (North Kesteven)

RT. HON. HENRY CHAPLIN (C)

1895—Rt Hon H. Chaplin (C)..		4653
W. S. Fox (R)..		2687
	Majority	1966
1892—Chaplin (C)		4157
Fox (R)		3250
	Majority	907

Representation Unchanged

Lincol

MR. H. F

1895—H. F.Polloc	
Halley Stew	
	M
1892—Stewart (R)	
Pollock (LU	
	M

Libe:

Lincolnshire, Stamford (See end of section)

Middlesex (Brentford)

MR. J. BIGWOOD (C)

1895—Unopposed
1892—J. Bigwood (C) 4417
    H. Heldman (R) 2625

    Majority 1792
    Representation Unchanged

Middlesex (Ealing)

LORD GEORGE HAMILTON (C)

1895—Unopposed
1892—Lord G. Hamilton (C) 5547
    Holman (R) 2112

    Majority 3435
    Representation Unchanged

CAPTAI

1895—Unoppos
1892—H. F. B
    H. Jones

    Re

Middlesex (Harrow)

MR. W. AMBROSE, Q.C. (C)

1895—Unopposed

1892—W. Ambrose (C) 6047
     T. Sadler (R) 3428

          Majority 2619
    Representation Unchanged

Middlesex (Hornsey)

MR. H. C. STEPHENS (C)

1895—Unopposed

1892—H. C. Stephens (C).. 6192
     Dr. Sydenham-Jones (R) 2913

          Majority 3279
    Representation Unchanged

Mi

MR. JO

1895—J. How:
    Clem Ec

1892—Howard
    Chance

      Re

Middlesex (Uxbridge)

SIR F. D. DIXON-HARTLAND (C)

1895—Unopposed

1892—Sir F. D. Dixon-Hartland (C) 5172
L. Probyn (R) 2029

Majority 3143

Representation Unchanged

.

Monmouthshire (North)

MR. R. MCKENNA (R)

1895—R. McKenna (R) 4965
W. Hume Williams (C).. 4203

Majority .. .. -762

1892—Price (R) 5020
Rolls (C) 3860

Majority 1160

Representation Unchanged

Mon

HON. F

1895—Hon F. C.
C. Cory (N

1892—Morgan (C
Baron Pro

Repr

Monmouthshire (West)	Norfolk (East)	MR. F.

RT. HON. SIR W. V. HARCOURT (R)

MR. R. J. PRICE (R)

1895—Rt Hon Sir W. V. Harcourt (R) .. 7043
W. E. Williams (C) 1956

Majority 5087

1892—Warmington (R) 7019
Meredyth (C) 1700

Majority 5319
Representation Unchanged

1895—R. J. Price (R) 4606
H. Rider Haggard (C) 4408

Majority 198

1892—Price (R) 4743
Birkbeck (C) 4303

Majority 440
Representation Unchanged

1895—F. W. Wil
R. T. Gur

1892—Higgins (
Majority,
Gurdon (
Majority,

Norfolk (North)	Norfolk (North-West)	
MR. H. H. COZENS-HARDY, Q.C. (R)	MR. JOSEPH ARCH (R)	MR.

1895—H. H. Cozens-Hardy (R) 4246	1895—J. Arch (R) 4817	1895—F. A.
Sir Kenneth-Kemp (C) 3738	E. Tighe (C) 3520	T. H.
Majority 508	Majority 1297	
1892—Cozens-Hardy (R) 4561	1892—Arch (R) 4911	1892—Taylor
Cator (C) 3278	Bentinck (C) 3822	Kitchi
Majority 1283	Majority 1089	
Representation Unchanged	Representation Unchanged	R

Norfolk (South-West)	**Northamptonshire (East)**	**Northa**
MR. T. L. HARE (C)	MR. F. A. CHANNING (R)	MR. J.

Norfolk (South-West)

'95—T. L. Hare (C) 3968
R. Winfrey (R) 3762

Majority 206

'92—Hare (C) 4077
Lee-Warner (R) 3739

Majority 338
Representation Unchanged

Northamptonshire (East)

1895—F. A. Channing (R) 6177
H. Lush-Wilson, Q.C. (C) 4961

Majority 1216

1892—Channing (R) 5827
Potter (C) 4346

Majority 1484
Representation Unchanged

Northamptonshire, North (See end of section)

Northa

1895—J. Pender (C
Rt Hon C. F

M

1892—Spencer (R)
Pender (C)..

M
Co

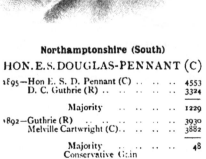

Northamptonshire (South)

HON. E. S. DOUGLAS-PENNANT (C)

1895—Hon E. S. D. Pennant (C)	4553
D. C. Guthrie (R)	3324
Majority	1229
1892—Guthrie (R)	3930
Melville Cartwright (C)..	3882
Majority	48
Conservative Gain	

Northumberland (Berwick-on-Tweed)

SIR E. GREY, BART. (R)

1895—Sir E. Grey (R)	4378
Lord Warkworth (C)	3593
Majority	785
1892—Grey (R)	4002
Askew-Robertson (C)	3560
Majority	442
Representation Unchanged	

Northu

MR. W.

1895—W. C. Beau	
C. E. Hunt	
1892—Clayton (C	
Majority, 8	
Clayton uns	
4804 : Clayt	
Repre	

Northumberland (Tyneside)	Northumberland (Wansbeck)	Nottingl
MR. J. A. PEASE (R)	MR. CHARLES FENWICK (R)	SIR FREDEl

<table>
<tr><td>1895—J. A. Pease (R)   6066
Arnold White (LU)   ..   ..   5631</td><td>1895—C. Fenwick (R)   5629
J. J. Harris (Lab-U)   ..   ..   ..   2422</td><td>1895—Sir F. Miln
R. E. Lead</td></tr>
<tr><td>Majority   ..   ..   ..   435</td><td>Majority   ..   ..   ..   3207</td><td>l</td></tr>
<tr><td>1892—Pease (R)   5468
White (LU)   ..   ..   5018</td><td>1892—Fenwick (R)   5696
Hill (LU) ..   ..   2920</td><td>1892—Milner (C).
Yoxall (R).</td></tr>
<tr><td>Majority   450
Representation Unchanged</td><td>Majority   2776
Representation Unchanged</td><td>Repre</td></tr>
</table>

Nottinghamshire, Mansfield (See end of section)   *Nottinghamshire, Newark (See end*

Nottinghamshire (Rushcliffe)
MR. J. E. ELLIS (R)

1895—J. E. Ellis (R)..	..	..	..	..	5752
G. M. Smith (LU)..	..	..	..	..	5119
	Majority	..	..	..	633
1892—Ellis (R)	..	..	..	..	5380
Seely (LU)	..	..	..	..	4588
	Majority	..	..	..	792
	Representation Unchanged				

Oxfordshire (Banbury)
MR. A. BRASSEY (C)

1895—A. Brassey (C)..	..	..	..	..	4057
C. Thornton (R)	..	..	..	..	3074
	Majority	..	..	..	983
1892—Samuelson (R)..	..	..	..	..	3640
Wynne (C)	..	..	..	..	3453
	Majority	..	..	..	187
	Conservative Gain				

MR. R.

1895—R. H.				
H. San				
1892—Parker				
Phillim				
R

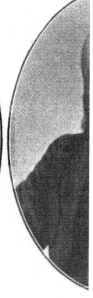

Oxfordshire (Woodstock)

MR. G. H. MORRELL (C)

1895—G. H. Morrell (C)	..	..	..	..	4669
G. R. Benson (R)	..	..	..	..	3740
	Majority	..	..	..	929
1892—Benson (R)	..	..	..	..	4278
Morrell (C)	..	..	..	..	4167
	Majority	..	..	..	111
	Conservative Gain				

Rutlandshire

MR. G. H. FINCH (C)

1895—Unopposed

1892—Unopposed

Representation Unchanged

Shro

MR. JAS

1895—Unopposed

1892—More (LU)
Morris (R)

M
Repres

Shropshire (Newport)

COL. W. KENYON-SLANEY (C)

1895—Unopposed

1892—Kenyon-Slaney (C).. 4815
    Lander (R) 3530

        Majority 1285
    Representation Unchanged

Shropshire (Oswestry)

MR. STANLEY LEIGHTON (C)

1895—Stanley Leighton (C) 4605
    Captain O. Thomas (R) 3598

        Majority 1007
1892—Leighton Unopposed
    Representation Unchanged

S

MR. A. H

1895—Unopp

1892—Brow
    Sande

Somersetshire (Bridgwater)

MR. E. J. STANLEY (C)

1895—Unopposed

1892—E. J. Stanley (C) 4555
     J. D. Walker (R) 3362

         Majority 1193
     Representation Unchanged

Somersetshire (East)

MR. HENRY HOBHOUSE (LU)

1895—H. Hobhouse (LU) 4408
     S. Hanham (R) 3334

         Majority 1074

1892—Hobhouse (LU) 4330
     Morley (R) 3575

         Majority 755
     Representation Unchanged

Somer

VISCOUNT

1895—Viscount Wey
     J. E. Barlow

         M

1892—Barlow (R)
     Lord Weymo

         M
     Co

Staffordshire (Burton)

MR. SYDNEY EVERSHED (R)

1895—Unopposed
1892—Unopposed
Representation Unchanged

Staffordshire (Handsworth)

SIR HENRY MEYSEY-THOMPSON,
BART. (LU)

1895—Unopposed
1892—Sir H. Meysey-Thompson (LU) 7370
    H. Gilzean Reid (R) 5433
                                 ————
          Majority 1937
      Representation Unchanged

Staffordsh

RT. HON. A.
Q

1895—Unopposed
1892—Rt Hon A. S.
    T. Parker (R)
          Maj
      Represen

Staffordshire (Leek)

MR. C. BILL (C)

1895—C. Bill (C)	..	4705
R. Pearce (R)	..	4091
Majority	..	614
1892—Bill (C)	..	4576
Nicholson (R)	..	4213
Majority	..	363

Representation Unchanged

Staffordshire (Lichfield)

MR. H. C. FULFORD (R)

1895—H. C. Fulford (R)	..	3902
Major Darwin (LU)	..	3858
Majority	..	44
1892—Darwin (LU)	..	3376
Swinburne (R)..	..	3572
Majority	..	4

Radical Gain

Staffor

MR.

1895—J. Heath		
L. K. Sho		
1892—Heath (C)		
Shoobridg		

Repr

Staffordshire (West)	Suffolk (Eye)	S
HON. H. A. BASS (LU)	MR. F. S. STEVENSON (R)	MR.

Suffolk (Stowmarket)

MR. J. MALCOLM (C)

1895—J. Malcolm (C)		5144
H. Walker (R)..		3701
Majority		1443
1892—Sidney Stern (R)		4630
Viscount Chelsea (C)		4486
Majority		144
Conservative Gain		

Suffolk (Sudbury)

MR. W. CUTHBERT QUILTER (LU)

1895—Unopposed		
1892—W. C. Quilter (LU)		5111
A. G. Ogilvie (R)		2905
Majority		2206
Representation Unchanged		

Suf

CAPTAIN

1895—Captain E.	
R. L. Eve	
1892—Everett (R	
Anstruther	

Surrey (Chertsey)

MR. G. H. COMBE (C)

1895—Unopposed
1892—Unopposed
Representation Unchanged

Surrey (Epsom)

MR. TOWNSEND BUCKNILL, Q.C.
(C)

1895—Unopposed
1892—T. Bucknill (C) 5123
    Hon T. A. Brassey (R).. 2723

        Majority 2400
    Representation Unchanged

S

HON. W. S

1895—Unoppos
1892—Hon W.
    G. Lawr

    Re

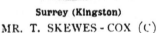

Surrey (Kingston)

MR. T. SKEWES - COX (C)

1895—T. Skewes-Cox (C)	5745
C. Burt (R)	3595
	Majority	2150
1892—Temple (C)	5100
Hodgson (R)	4357
	Majority	743
	Representation Unchanged	

Surrey (Reigate)

HON. H. CUBITT (C)

1895—Unopposed	
1892—Hon H. Cubitt (C)	4786
F. E. Barnes (R)	3097
	Majority	1689
	Representation Unchanged	

Sur

MR. H. CO

1895—Unopposed
1892—H. Cosmo
T. A. Mea

Repr

Sussex (Chichester)

LORD E. TALBOT (C)

1895—Unopposed

1892—Lord W. Lennox (C), 4236; Reid (R), 2361:
Majority, 1875. Bye-election (Aug., 1894)—
Lord E. Talbot, Unopposed

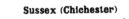

Representation Unchanged

Sussex (Eastbourne)

VICE-ADMIRAL E. FIELD (C)

1895—Admiral Field (C)	4139
Captain the Hon T. S. Brand (R)	4079
Majority	60
1892—Field (C)	4037
Brand (R)	3674
Majority	363

Representation Unchanged

S

MR. G

1895—Mr. (
C. Co

1892—Gath
Jenk

Sussex (Horsham)

MR. J. HEYWOOD JOHNSTONE (C)

1895—Unopposed

1892—Sir W. Barttelot (C), 4303; R. G. Wilberforce (R), 2268: Majority, 2035. Bye-Election (February, 1893)—Johnstone (C), 4150; Wilberforce (R), 2666: Majority, 1484

Representation Unchanged

Sussex (Lewes)

SIR HENRY FLETCHER, BART. (C)

1895—Unopposed

1892—Sir H. Fletcher (C)..	..	..	..	..	..	5621
Henry Prince (R)	..	..	..	..	..	2322
Majority	..	..	..	..	3299

Representation Unchanged

S

MR. A. M.

1895—Unopposed

1892—A. M. Brook
G. M. Ball (

M

Represe

Warwickshire (Nuneaton)

MR. F. A. NEWDIGATE (C)

1895—F. A. Newdigate (C)	.. ..	5572
J. Tomkinson (R)	.. ..	4175
	Majority	1397
1892—Newdigate (C)..	.. ..	4899
Vero (R)	.. ..	4258
	Majority	641

Representation Unchanged

Warwickshire (Rugby)

HON. R. G. VERNEY (C)

1895—Hon R. G. Verney (C) ..	.. .. ..	4354
J. C. Grant (R)	.. ..	4070
	Majority	284
1892—Cobb (R) ..	.. ..	4519
Galloway (C)	.. .., ..	3831
	Majority	688

Conservative Gain

Warwick

MR. P.

1895—Unopposed	
1892—P. A. Muntz	
W. Johnson (	
	M
	Represe

Warwickshire, S

Westmorland (Appleby)	Westmorland (Kendal)	W
SIR J. SAVORY, BART. (C)	CAPTAIN J. F. BAGOT (C)	MR. A. H

<table>
<tr><td>1895—Sir J. Savory (C) 2950
T. W. Fry (R).. .. .. 2077</td><td>1895—Captain J. F. Bagot (C) 2771
H. Stephenson (R).. .. .. .. 2049</td><td>1895—A. Hopk
Lord E.</td></tr>
<tr><td>Majority .. .. .. 873</td><td>Majority .. .. .. 722</td><td></td></tr>
<tr><td>1892—Savory (C).. 2963
Tufton (R) .. .. 2256</td><td>1892—Bagot (C) 2838
Farrar (R).. .. .. 2209</td><td>1892—Husband
Story-M</td></tr>
<tr><td>Majority 707
Representation Unchanged</td><td>Majority 629
Representation Unchanged</td><td>I</td></tr>
</table>

Wiltshire, Chippenham (See end of section)

Wiltshire (Devizes)

MR. E. A. GOULDING (C)

1895—E. A. Goulding (C)	.. ..	4114
C. E. Hobhouse (R)	.. ..	3637
	Majority	.. ..	477
1892—Hobhouse (R)	.. ..	3896
Long (C)	.. ..	3758
	Majority	.. ..	138
	Conservative Gain		

Wiltshire (Westbury)

CAPTAIN CHALONER (C)

1895—Captain Chaloner (C)	.. ..	4497
G. P. Fuller (R)	.. ..	4331
	Majority	.. ..	166
1892—Fuller (R) ..	.. ..	4554
Laverton (C)	.. ..	3930
	Majority	.. ..	624
	Conservative Gain		

W

VISCOUN

1895—Viscount
L. E. Pyk

1892—Viscount
Sir T. Gr

Rep

Worcestershire (Bewdley)

MR. A. BALDWIN (C)

1895—Unopposed
1892—Unopposed
Representation Unchanged

Worcestershire (Droitwich)

MR. R. BIDDULPH MARTIN (LU)

1895—Unopposed

1892—R. B. Martin (LU)					3980
T. Stephens (R)					3410
Majority					570
Representation Unchanged					

Wo

MR. J. AU

1895—Unoppose

1892—J. Austen
Oscar Bro

Rep

Worcestershire (Evesham)

LT-COL. C. W. LONG (C)

1895—Unopposed

1892—Lechmere (C), 4170; Impey (R), 3590: Majority, 580. Bye-election (Jan., 1895)— Long (C), 4760; Impey (R), 3585: Majority, 1175

Representation Unchanged

Worcestershire (North)

MR. J. W. WILSON (LU)

1895—J. W. Wilson (LU)					5012
R. Waite (R)					4024
Majority					988
1892—Hingley (R)					5329
Bridgman (LU)					3171
Majority					2158

Liberal Unionist Gain

Yorksh

COLONEL R

1895—Unopposed

1892—Colonel R.
A. W. Scarr

M
Repre

Yorkshire (Barnsley)
EARL COMPTON (R)

1895—Earl Compton (R)		6820
Colonel the Hon R. Greville (LU)	..	4653
Majority		2167
1892—Earl Compton (R)		6739
Foljambe (LU)		3498
Majority		3241

Representation Unchanged

Yorkshire (Buckrose)
MR. ANGUS HOLDEN (R)

1895—A. Holden (R)		4076
T. C. Goff (C)		3986
Majority		90
1892—Holden (R)		4294
Fison (C)		3642
Majority		652

Representation Unchanged

Yor
MR. H.

1895—H. F. Pea	
Lieut-Colo	
1892—Pease (R)	
Dorman (	

Repr

Yorkshire (Colne Valley)

SIR J. KITSON (R)

1895—Sir J. Kitson (R)	.. ..	4276
H. Thomas (LU)	.. ..	3737
T. Mann (Soc)	.. ..	1245
	Majority	.. .. ..	539
1892—Kitson (R)	.. ..	4987
Sugden (LU)	.. ..	4281
	Majority	.. .. ..	706

Representation Unchanged

Yorkshire (Doncaster)

MR. F. W. FISON (C)

1895—F. W. Fison (C)	.. ..	6098
J. Walton (R)	.. ..	5957
	Majority	.. .. ..	141
1892—Fleming (R)	.. ..	5831
Fitzwilliam (C)	.. ..	5552
	Majority	.. .. ..	279

Conservative Gain

York

MR. THOM

1895—T. Wayman (		
A. T. Clay (C		
	M	
1892—Wayman (R)		
Hope (C)		
	M	

Represe

Yorkshire (Hallamshire)

SIR F. T. MAPPIN, BART. (R)

1895—Sir F. T. Mappin (R)	..	..	..	5949
F. S. Hatchard (C)	..	..	..	5054
	Majority	..	.. ..	895

1892—Mappin Unopposed

Representation Unchanged

Yorkshire (Holderness)

CAPT. G. R. BETHELL (C)

1895—Captain G. R. Bethell (C)	..	..	..	4512
B. Hawksley (R)	..	..	..	3485
	Majority	..	.. ..	1027
1895—Bethell (C)	..	..	..	4158
Anderson (R)	..	..	..	3693
	Majority	..	.. ..	465

Representation Unchanged

Yor

MR. H

1895—H. J. Wi

G. E. Ra

1892—Wilson(R

Thomas (

Rep

Yorkshire (Howdenshire,

OL. W. H. WILSON-TODD (C)

5—Unopposed

2—Coi Wilson-Todd (C) 3998
   J. T. Woodhouse (R) 3648

      Majority 350
   Representation Unchanged

...... (Keighley)

MR. J. BRIGG (R)

1895—J. Brigg (R) 5036
   W. Bairstow (U) 4196

      Majority 840
1892—Holden (R) Unopposed
   Representation Unchanged

Yorks

MR. A. E

1895—A. E. Hutton
   W. Carr (C)

      Maj
1892—Hutton (R)
   Carr (C) ..

      Maj
   Represen

Yorkshire (Normanton)

MR. B. PICKARD (R)

1895—B. Pickard (R)..	5499
D'Arcy Wilson (C)..	3941
Majority	1558
1892—Pickard (R)	6134
Tew (C)	3803
Majority	2331
Representation Unchanged	

Yorkshire (Osgoldcross)

SIR JOHN AUSTIN, BART. (R)

1895—Sir J. Austin (R)	5119
J. Harling (C)..	4054
Majority	1065
1892—Austin (R)..	5160
Dobson (C)	3284
Majority	1876
Representation Unchanged	

Y•

MR. M. D

1895—M. D'Arcy
Sir J. Barr

1895--Barran (R)
D'Arcy W

Yorkshire (Pudsey)

MR. BRIGGS PRIESTLEY (R)

1895—B. Priestley (R)	.. ..	5540
Sir A. Fairbairn (LU)	.. ..	5070
	Majority	470
1892—Priestley (R)	.. ..	5523
Woodhouse (C)	.. ..	4924
	Majority	599
	Representation Unchanged	

Yorkshire (Richmond)

MR. J. HUTTON (C)

1895—J. Hutton (C)	.. ..	4555
E. R. Turton (R)	.. ..	3971
	Majority	584
1892—Elliot (C)	.. ..	4340
Turton (R)	.. ..	4181
	Majority	159
	Representation Unchanged	

Yo

MR. J. I

1895—J. L. Whar	
R. C. Philli	
	M
1892—Wharton (C	
Leetham (R	
	M
Repre:	

Yorkshire (Rotherham)

RT. HON. A. H. DYKE-ACLAND (R)

1895—Unopposed

1892—Dyke-Acland (R) 6567
Foljambe (LU) 2839

Majority 3728

Representation Unchanged

Yorkshire (Shipley)

MR. FORTESCUE FLANNERY (LU)

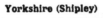

1895—F. Flannery (LU) 5999
W. P. Byles (R) 5921

Majority 78

1892—Byles (R) 5746
Peel (LU) 5464

Majority 282
Liberal Unionist Gain

Y⋯

MR. W⋯

1895—W. Morri⋯
J. A. Far⋯

1872—Roundell⋯
Morrison⋯

L⋯

Yorkshire (Sowerby)

RT. HON. J. W MELLOR (R)

1895—Rt Hon J. W. Mellor (R)	5328
J. Baily (LU)	3654
Majority	1674
1892—Mellor (R)..	5754
Crook (LU)	3324
Majority	2430

Representation Unchanged

Yorkshire (Spen Valley)

MR. T. P. WHITTAKER (R)

1895—T. P. Whittaker (R)	4700
F. Ellis (C)	3879
Majority	821
1892—Whittaker (R)	4952
Ellis (C)	3404
Majority	1548

Representation Unchanged

Yorkshi

MR. JOHN

1895—Unoppose
1892—Lawson (C
Reckitt (L

Repr

Yorkshire (Whitby)

MR. E. W. BECKETT (C)

1895—Unopposed

1892—E. W. Beckett (C)	4909
H. F. Pyman (R)	3826
Majority	1083

Representation Unchanged

Bedfordshire (Biggleswade)

LORD ALWYNE COMPTON (LU)

1895—Lord A. Compton (LU)..	5643
G. W. E. Russell (R)	5376
Majority	267
1892—Russell (R)	5600
Viscount Baring (LU)	5056
Majority	544

Liberal Unionist Gain

Derbyshire (North-East)

MR. T. D. BOLTON (R)

1895—T. D. Bolton (R)	4737
Dr. J. Court (LU)	4210
Majority	527
1892—Bolton (R)..	5206
Barnes (C)..	3036
Majority	2170

Representation Unchanged

Essex (Maldon)

HON. C. H. STRUTT (C)

1895—Hon C. H. Strutt (C) .. .. :.	4618
C. Dodd, Q.C. (R)..	4008
Majority	610
1892—Dodd (R)	4321
Gray (C)	4153
Majority	168

Conservative Gain

Esse

MR. A. MOI

1895—A. M. Wigram	
J. H. Bethell	
Maj	
1892—Theobald (C),	
Majority, 1182	
—Wigram (C	
Majority, 683	

Represen

Lanca

LORD B

1895—Unopposed

1892—Lt-Gen Feild
Hon Member
dissolution of
was returned

Represe

Lancashi

LORD S

1895—Unopposed

1892—Lord Stanley
L. Haslam (R

Ma

Represe

Leicestershire (Loughborough)
MR. E. JOHNSON-FERGUSON (R)

1895—E. Johnson-Ferguson (R)		4732
R. L. Tooth (C)		4360
Majority		372
1892—Ferguson (R)		4715
De Lisle (C)		3994
Majority		721

Representation Unchanged

Lincolnshire (Stamford)
MR. W. YOUNGER (C)

1895—W. Younger (C)		4203
A. Priestley (R)		3814
Majority		389
1892—Cust (C)		4150
Priestley (R)		4026
Majority		124

Representation Unchanged

Northamptonshire (North)
MR. E. P. MONCKTON (C)

1895—Unopposed

1892—Rt Hon Lord Burghley (C)		4505
J. T. Stockburn (R)		3823
Majority		682

Representation Unchanged

Nottinghamshire (Mansfield)
MR. J. CARVELL WILLIAMS (R)

1895—J. C. Williams (R)		5670
Col Eyre (C)		4285
Majority		1385
1892—Williams (R)		5731
Wardle (C)		3235
Majority		2496

Representation Unchanged

Nottinghamshire (Newark)
HON. H. FINCH HATTON (C)

1895—H. Finch Hatton, Unopposed
1892—Lord Newark, Unopposed

Representation Unchanged

Somersetshire (Wells)
HON. G. HYLTON-JOLLIFFE (C)

1895—Hon G. Hylton-Jolliffe (C)		4696
B. Morice (R)		3286
Majority		1410
1892—Paget (C)		4335
Morice (R)		3395
Majority		940

Representation Unchanged

Wal
COLON

1895—Colonel		
T. Sadle		
1892—Mitford		
Warmin		

Re

Wil
SIR J. DICI

1895—Sir J. D		
J. Thorn		
1892—Poynder		
Fuller (F		

Re

Cardiff District

Carmarthen District

MR. J. M. MACLEAN (C)

SIR J. J. JENKINS (LU)

1895—J. M. Maclean (C)	.. ..	8386	
Sir E. J. Reed (R)	.. ..	7562	
	Majority	.. ..	824
1892—Reed (R)	.. ..	7226	
Gunn (LU)	.. .. ..	6540	
	Majority	.. ..	686
	Conservative Gain		

1895—Sir J. J. Jenkins (LU)	.. ..	
Major Jones (R)	.. ..	
	Majority	
1892—Jones (R)	.. ..	
Jenkins (LU)	.. ..	
	Majority	
	Liberal	

Denbigh District	**Flint District**	**MR. I**
MR. W. T. HOWELL (C)	MR. J. H. LEWIS (R)	

Merthyr Tydvil
MR. W. P. MORGAN (R)

1895—D. A. Thomas (R)	.. ..	9250
W. P. Morgan (R)	.. ..	8554
H. C. Lewis (C)	.. ..	6525
Allen Upward (Lab)	.. .. ..	659
	Majority	2029

1892—Thomas (R), 11948; Morgan (R), 11756;
Williams (C), 2304: Majority, 9452
Representation Unchanged

Montgomery District
MAJOR E. PRYCE JONES (C)

1895—Major E. Pryce Jones (C)	.. .. ..	1435
O. Philipps (R)	.. ..	1351
	Majority	84
1892—Jones (C)	.. ..	1400
Tracy (R)	.. ..	1288
	Majority	112

Representation Unchanged

Pembroke
LIEUT.-G

1895—Lieut.-G	
C. F. E.	
1892—Allen (R)	
Laurie (C	

Swansea District

MR. D. BRYNMOR JONES (R)

1895—D. B. Jones (R) 3850
—. Headley (Lab) 2018
Col. Wright (C) 1851

    Majority 1999

1892—Vivian (R), 5959 ; Monger (LU), 933
Majority, 5026. Bye-election (June, 1893)—
William Williams (R) Unopposed
Representation Unchanged

Swansea Town

SIR J. T. D. LLEWELYN, BART. (

1895—Sir J. T. D. Llewelyn (C) 3ᵢ
R. J. Burnie (R) 3

    Majority .. ..

1892—Burnie (R).. 3
Llewelyn (C) 3ᵢ

    Majority .. ..
Conservative Gain

Anglesey
MR. E. J. GRIFFITH (R)

1895—E. J. Griffith (R)	4224
J. R. Roberts (C)	3197
Majority	1027
1892—Lewis (R)	4420
Lloyd (LU)	2702
Majority	1718
Representation Unchanged	

Brecknockshire
MR. C. MORLEY (R)

1895—C. Morley (R)	4594
Col. T. Wood (C)	3451
Majority	1143
1892—Maitland (R)	4676
Wood (C)	3418
Majority	1258
Representation Unchanged	

Ca[...]
MR. AB[...]

1895—A. Thom[...]
J. E. Ri[...]
1892—Thomas [...]
Davies [...]
Re[...]

Cardiganshire (See end of section)

Carmarthenshire (West)	**Carnarvonshire (South)**	**D**
MR. J. L. MORGAN (R)	MR. J. BRYN ROBERTS (R)	SIR G.

1895—J. L. Morgan (R) 4143
W. J. Buckley (LU) 3103

Majority 1040

1892—Morgan Unopposed

Representation Unchanged

1895—Unopposed

1892—Roberts (R) 4567
Humphreys (C) 1973

Majority 2594

Representation Unchanged

1895—Sir G. O
H. St. J

1892—Morgan
Watkin

Re

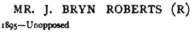

Carnarvonshire North (See end of section)

Denbighshire (West,

MR. J. H. ROBERTS (R)

1895—J. H. Roberts (R)	..	.. ..	4481
Captain W. Edwards (C)		.. .. ..	2878
	Majority	.. .. ..	1603
1892—Roberts (R)	..	.. ..	4612
Cornwallis West (LU)	..	.. .. ..	2279
	Majority	.. .. ..	2333
	Representation Unchanged		

Flintshire

MR. S. SMITH (R)

1895—S. Smith (R)	..	.. ..	4376
Colonel Howard (C)		.. .. ..	3925
	Majority	.. .. ..	451
1892—Smith (R)	..	.. ..	4597
Cunliffe (LU)	..	.. .. ..	3145
	Majority	.. .. ..	1452
	Representation Unchanged		

Gl

MR. A

1895—A. Thom		
C. J. Ja		
1892—Thomas		
Lewis (C		
	Re	

Glamorganshire (Mid)	Glamorganshire (Rhonnda)	Glam
MR. S. T. EVANS (R)	MR. W. ABRAHAMS (R)	MR. I

Glamorganshire (Mid)

MR. S. T. EVANS (R)

1895—S. T. Evans (R) 5612
    J. E. Vaughan (C) 2935

        Majority 2677

1892—Evans (R) 5941
    Grove (C) 1725

        Majority 4216
    Representation Unchanged

Glamorganshire (Rhonnda)

MR. W. ABRAHAMS (R)

1895—Unopposed
1892—Unopposed
Representation Unchanged

Glam

MR. I

1895—D Randell
    C. H. Gas

1892—Randell U
    Repr

Glamorganshire, South (See end of section)

	Merionethshire		Montgomeryshire		MR.

Merionethshire
MR. T. E. ELLIS (R)

1895—T. E. Ellis (R)..	..	..	..	..	5173
C. E. J. Owen (C) ..	..	..	..	..	2232

Majority	..	..	..	2941

1892—Ellis (R)	..	..	..	..	5178
Owen (C) ..	..	..	..	..	1937

Majority	..	..	..	3241

Representation Unchanged

Montgomeryshire
MR. A. C. HUMPHREY OWEN (R)

1895—A. C. H. Owen (R)	..	..	..	3442
R. W. Wynn (C)	..	..	..	3415

Majority	..	..	..	27

1892 — Rendel (R), 3662; Mytton (C), 2847:
Majority, 815. Bye-election (March, 1894)—
Owen (R), 3440; Wynn (C), 3215: Majority,
225

Representation Unchanged

MR. W. R. D

1895—W. R. D	
A. S. Da	

1892—Davies (R	
Phillips (	

Re

Cardiganshire
MR. V. DAVIES (R)

1895—V. Davies (R) .. .. 4(
    J. Harford (C).. .. .. 3;

        Majority 1

1892—Rowlands (R), 5249; Jones (LU), 32;
    Majority, 1971. Bye-election (1893)—R<
    lands (R), Unopposed

    Representation Unchanged

Carnarvonshire (North)
MR. W. JONES (R)

1895—W. Jones (R) 4;
    Prof. A. Hughes (C) 2;

        Majority .. .. 1(

1892—W. Rathbone (R) Unopposed

    Representation Unchanged

Radnorshire
MR. W. P. MILBANK (C)

1895—W. P. Milbank (C) 1049
    F. Edwards (R) 1868

        Majority 81

1892—Edwards (R) 1973
    Bradney (C) 1740

        Majority 233
    Conservative Gain

Glamorganshire (South)
MAJOR W. H. WYNDHAM - QUI
(LU)

1895—Major W-Quin (LU) 5
    A. J. Williams (R).. 4

        Majority .. ..

1892—Williams (R) 4
    Morgan (C) 3

        Majority .. ..
    Liberal Unionist Gain

Aberdeen (North)
MR. W. A. HUNTER (R)

1895—W. A. Hunter (R)	4156
J. L. Mahon (Lab)..	608
Majority	3548
1892—Hunter (R)	4462
Lee (LU)	870
Majority	3592
Representation Unchanged	

Aberdeen (South)
THE RT. HON. J. BRYCE (R)

1895—The Rt Hon J. Bryce (R)	3985
D. Stewart (LU)	3121
Majority	864
1892—Bryce (R)	3513
McCullagh (U)	1768
Champion (Lab)	991
Majority	1745
Representation Unchanged	

MR. C.

1895—C. L. O	
W. Birk	
1892—Birkmyr	
I. Some	

Dumfries District
SIR R. T. REID, Q.C. (R)

1895—Sir R. T. Reid (R)			1785
W. Murray (LU)			1185
	Majority		600
1892—Reid (R)			1698
Agnew (C)			1168
	Majority		530

Representation Unchanged

Dundee
SIR JOHN LENG (R)

1895—E. Robertson (R)			7602
Sir J. Leng (R)			7592
W. C. Smith (LU)			5390
E. Jenkins (C)			4318
J. Macdonald (Lab)			1313
	Majority		2202

1892—Leng (R), 8484 ; Robertson (R), 8191 ;
Ogilvy Dalgleish (C), 5659 ; Smith (LU),
5066 ; Macdonald (Lab), 354 : Majority, 2825
Representation Unchanged

MR. E[

1895—E. R	
Sir J	
E. J	
J. M	

1892—Leng
Ogilv
5066

Edinburgh (Central)

MR. W. McEWAN (R)

1895—Unopposed

1892—McEwan (R) 3733
Connell (LU) 1758
Wilson (Lab) 438
———
Majority 1975
Representation Unchanged

Edinburgh (East)

DR. ROBERT WALLACE (R)

1895—R. Wallace (R) 3499
H. G. Younger (LU) 3050
———
Majority 449
1892—Wallace (R) 3963
Fullarton (LU) 2803
———
Majority 1160
Representation Unchanged

Edin

MR. R

1895—R. Cox (LU)
H. W. Paul

M

1892—Paul (R) ..
McIver (LU)

M
Libe

Edinburgh (West)
MR. LEWIS McIVER (LU)

1895—Unopposed

1892 — Viscount Wolmer (LU), 3728; T. R.
Buchanan (R), 3216: Majority, 512. Bye-
election (1895)—Lewis McIver (LU), 3782;
The Master of Elibank (R), 3075: Majority,
707

Representation Unchanged

Elgin District
MR. A. ASHER, Q.C. (R)

1895—A. Asher (R) 1853
C. G. Gordon (LU) 1161

Majority 692

1892—Asher (R) 1668
Grant (LU) 1127

Majority 541
Representation Unchanged

Falkirk District (See end of section)

Glasg
MR. A. I

1895—A. D. Prova
A. Stuart (L
Shaw Maxw

M

1892—Provand (R)
Stuart (C) ..

M
Represe

Glasgow (Bridgeton)

RT. HON. SIR G. TREVELYAN (R)

1895—Rt Hon Sir G. Trevelyan (R)	3161
C. S. Dickson (C)	2719
J. S. Watson (Lab)	609
Majority	442
1892—Trevelyan (R)	4654
Maughan (C)	3253
Majority	1401

Representation Unchanged

Glasgow (Camlachie)

MR. ALEXANDER CROSS (LU)

1895—A. Cross (LU)	3198
S. Chisholm (R)	2497
R. Smellie (Lab)	696
Majority	701
1892—Cross (LU)	3455
McCulloch (R)..	3084
Cunninghame Graham (Lab)	906
Watt (Lab)	179
Majority	371

Representation Unchanged

Gl

MR. J.

1895—J. G. A. B	
E. A. Ada	
1892—Baird (C)	
Menzies (I	

Rep

Glasgow (College Division)
SIR J. STIRLING MAXWELL, BART. (C)

1895—Sir J. S. Maxwell (C)	..	..	..	5364
Sir C. Cameron, Bart. (R)	..	..	..	4219
Majority	..	..	..	1145
1892—Cameron (R)	..	..	..	5804
Maxwell (C)	..	..	..	4758
Brodie (Lab)	..	..	..	225
Majority	..	..	..	1046
Conservative Gain				

Glasgow (St. Rollox)
MR. F. FAITHFULL BEGG (C)

1895—F. Faithfull Begg (C)	..	..	..	4561
Sir J. M. Carmichael, Bart. (R)	..	..	4200
J. E. Woolacot (Lab)	..	..	..	405
Majority	..	..	..	361
1892—Carmichael (R)	..	..	..	6247
Elliott (LU)	..	..	..	4891
Majority	..	..	..	1356
Conservative Gain				

Glas
MR. A. CAM

1895—A. C. Corb		
G. Green (I		
F. Smith (I		
1892—Corbett (L		
Caldwell (I		
Bennett Bu		
Repr		

Greenock

SIR T. SUTHERLAND (LU)

1895—Sir T. Sutherland (LU)	3571
A. E. Fletcher (R)	2753
Majority	818
1892—Sutherland (LU)	2942
Bruce (R)	2887
Majority	55

Representation Unchanged

Hawick District

MR. THOMAS SHAW (R)

1895—T. Shaw (R)	3033
J. Saunderson (LU)	2531
Majority	502

1892—Shaw (R), 3004; Watson (LU), 2639: Majority, 365. Bye-election (March, 1894—on Mr. Shaw's appointment as Solicitor-General)—Shaw, 3203; Fullarton (LU), 2556: Majority, 647
　　　Representation Unchanged

MR. R

1895—R. B.
　　　H. B

1892—Beith
　　　Finla

Kilmarnock District	Kirkcaldy District	L...
COLONEL J. M. DENNY (C)	MR. J. H. DALZIEL (R)	MR. R. C. MU...

1895—Colonel J. M. Denny (C)	 5432	1895—J. H. Dalziel (R) 3078	1895—R. C. Munr...
Stephen Williamson (R)	 5051	C. J. Kekewich (C) 1122	J. Wilson (L...
Majority 381	Majority 1956	M...
1892—Williamson (R) 5110	1892—Dalziel (R) 2741	1892—Fergusson (...
Dickson (C) 4335	Chisholm (C) 939	Majority, 16,...
		—Fergusson
Majority 775	Majority 1802	Majority, 11...
Conservative Gain	Representation Unchanged	

Montrose District

MR. J. SHIRESS WILL, Q.C. (R)

1895—J. S. Will (R) 3594
     G. W. Baxter (LU).. 2462

           Majority 1132

1892—Will (R) 3941
     Lockhart (LU).. 2090

           Majority 1851
     Representation Unchanged

Paisley

SIR W. DUNN (R)

1895—Sir W. Dunn (R) 4404
     A. Moffatt (C) 3062

           Majority 1342

1892—Dunn (R) 4262
     Johnston (C) 2441

           Majority 1821
     Representation Unchanged

MR.

1895—R. Wal
     W. Wh

1892—Whitel
     Parker
     Woolle

Stirling District

T. HON. SIR H. CAMPBELL-
BANNERMAN (R)

95—Rt Hon Sir H. C.-Bannerman (R)	..	2786
S. McCaskie (C)	..	1653
Majority	..	1133
92—Campbell-Bannerman (R) ..	..	2791
Hughes (LU)	..	1695
Majority	..	1096
Representation Unchanged		

St. Andrews Burghs

MR. H. T. ANSTRUTHER (LU)

1895—H. T. Anstruther (LU)..	..	1185
J. Paton (R)	..	989
Majority	..	196
1892—Anstruther (LU)	..	1064
Martin-White (R)	..	954
Majority	..	110
Representation Unchanged		

Wl

SIR JOHN

1895—Sir J. Pender	
T. C. Hedder	
Ma	
1892—Pender (LU)	
Cameron (R)	
Ma	
Represei	

Falkirk District

MR. J. WILSON (LU)

1895—J. Wilson (LU) 4075
      H. Smith (R) 3822

          Majority 253

1892—Smith (R) 3816
      Sinclair (LU) 3177

          Majority 639
          Liberal Unionist Gain

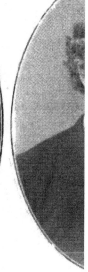

Aberdeenshire (East)
MR. T. R. BUCHANAN (R)

1895—T. R. Buchanan (R) 4723
W. Smith (LU) 3308
—————
Majority 1415

1892—Esslemont (R), 5116; Colonel Russell (LU),
3492: Majority, 1624. Bye-election (Decem-
ber, 1892) — Buchanan (R), 4243; Russell
(LU), 2917: Majority, 1326
Representation Unchanged

Aberdeenshire (West)
DR. R. FARQUHARSON (R)

1895—R. Farquharson (R) 4187
Sir A. H. Grant, Bart (LU) 3967
—————
Majority 220

1892—Farquharson (R) 3720
Grant (LU) 3640
—————
Majority 80
Representation Unchanged

MR.

1895—D. N. N
Sir D. H

1892—Macfarla
Malcolm

Ayrshire (North)

HON. THOMAS COCHRANE (LU)

1895—Hon T. Cochrane (LU)		5612
W. Robertson (R)		4902
Majority		710
1892—Cochrane (LU)..		5346
Wedderburn (R)		4898
Majority		448

Representation Unchanged

Ayrshire (South)

SIR WILLIAM ARROL (LU)

1895—Sir W. Arrol (LU)		6875
Eugene Wason (R)..		6325
Majority		550
1892—Wason (R)..		6535
Arrol (LU)..		6338
Majority		197

Liberal Unionist Gain

SIR WILL

1895—Sir W. We		
J. A. Gran		
1892—Duff (R),		
869. Bye		
burn (R		
771		

Berwickshire

MR. ——————

1895 ——

Fifeshire

A. G. —————— MURRAY (C)

—Unop——

—A. —————— 1466
R. —————— 1013

.. 453

Unchanged

DR. ——

Clackmannan & Kinross	**Dumbartonshire**
RT. HON. J. B. BALFOUR, Q.C. (R)	MR. A. WYLIE (C)

1895—Rt Hon J. B. Balfour (R) 3133
   G. Younger (C) 2588

          Majority 545

1892—Balfour (R) 3541
   Aitchison (LU) 1927

          Majority 1614
          Representation Unchanged

1895—A. Wylie (C) 5375
   Captain Sinclair (R) 5342

          Majority 33

1892—Sinclair (R) 5249
   Wylie (C) 4956

          Majority 293
          Conservative Gain

MR. A.

1895—A. R. Sou
   W. J. Ma

1892—Maxwell (
   McKie (R

Elgin and Nairn (See end of section)

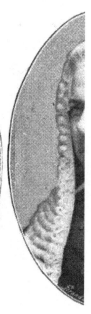

Fifeshire (East)	Fifeshire (West)	H
RT. HON. H. H. ASQUITH, Q.C. (R)	MR. AUGUSTINE BIRRELL, Q.C. (R)	MR. R. B.

Fifeshire (East)

RT. HON. H. H. ASQUITH, Q.C. (R)

1895—H. H. Asquith (R) 4332
J. Gilmour (C) 3616

Majority 716

1892—Asquith (R) 3743
Gilmour (C) 3449

Majority 294
Representation Unchanged

Fifeshire (West)

MR. AUGUSTINE BIRRELL, Q.C. (R)

1895—A. Birrell (R) 4719
R. G. Erskine-Wemyss (LU) 2965

Majority 1754

1892—Birrell (R) 5215
Yellowlees (LU) 1633

Majority 3582
Representation Unchanged

H

MR. R. B.

1895—R. B. Hald
Master of F

1892—Haldane (R
Master of F

Repre

Forfarshire (See end of section)

Inverness-shire	Kincardineshire	Kir
MR. J. BAILLIE (C)	MR. J. W. CROMBIE (R)	SIR MAR

Lanarkshire (Mid)	Lanarkshire (Partick)	La
MR. J. CALDWELL (R)	MR. J. PARKER SMITH (LU)	MR. J

1895—J. Caldwell (R) **4447**
C. K. Mackenzie (LU) **4375**

Majority **71**

1892— Phillips (R), 4611 ; Stuart (C), 3489 :
Majority, 1122. Bye-election (April, 1894)—
Caldwell (R), 3965 ; Stuart (C), 3635 ;
Smellie (Lab), 1221: Majority, 330
Representation Unchanged

Lanarkshire, Govan (See end of section)

1895—J. Parker Smith (LU) **5551**
L. Mackenzie (R) **4344**

Majority **1207**

1892—Parker Smith (LU).. .. .. **5005**
Tennant (R) **4278**

Majority **727**
Representation Unchanged

Lanarkshire, North-East (See end of section)

1895—J. H. Ho₂
R. Lambi

1892—Hozier (C
Hedderwi

Repi

Lanarkshire, I

Linlithgowshire

MR. ALEXANDER URE (R)

1895—A. Ure (R) 3760
Captain T. Hope (C) 3153

Majority .. .. .. 60·

1892—Maclagan (R) 2870; Hope (C), 2709
Majority, 161. Bye-election (June, 1893)—
Hope (C), 3230; Ure (R), 3071: Majority, 159
Radical Gain

Midlothian

SIR T. D. GIBSON CARMICHAEL, BT.
(R)

1895—Sir T. D. G. Carmichael (R) 6090
Major the Hon. North Dalrymple(LU) 5631

Majority 459

1892—Rt Hon W. E. Gladstone (R) 5845
Colonel Wauchope (C) 5155

Majority 690
Representation Unchanged

MR. WA

1895—W. Th
Maste

1895—Thorb
Carmi

Perthshire (East

SIR JOHN KINLOCH, BART. (R)

1895—Sir John Kinloch (R)	3410
W. L. Boase (C)	2535
Majority	875
1892—Kinloch (R)	353?
Boase (C)	2484
Majority	1049
Representation Unchanged	

Perthshire (West)

SIR DONALD CURRIE (LU)

1895—Sir D. Currie (LU)	3379
J. D. Hope (R)	3087
Majority	292
1892—Currie (LU)	3422
Ure (R)	3053
Majority	369
Representation Unchanged	

Re

MR. H. S

1895—Unoppose

1892—H. Shaw
J. Murdo

Rep

Renfrewshire (West)

MR. C. BINE RENSHAW (C)

1895—C. B. Renshaw (C)	..	..	..	3909
Captain D. V. Pirie (R)	..	..	..	3397
	Majority	..	..	512
˙92—Renshaw (C)	..	..	..	3773
R. Wallace (R)	..	..	..	3322
	Majority	..	..	451
	Representation Unchanged			

Ross & Cromarty

MR. J. GALLOWAY WEIR (R)

1895—J. G. Weir (R)	..	..	..	3272
Major Jackson (LU)	..	..	..	2409
	Majority	..	..	863
1892—Weir (R)	..	..	..	3171
McLean (LU)	..	..	..	2413
	Majority	..	..	758
	Representatior Unchanged			

Ro

EARL OF

| 1895—Lord Dalkeit |
| Hon. M. F. |
| | Ma |
| 1892—Napier (R) |
| Elliott (LU) |
| | Ma |
| Co |

Stirlingshire

MR. J. M. MCKILLOP (LU)

1895—J. McKillop (LU)	..	..	..	..	..	5916
W. Jacks (R)	..	..	.:	..	..	5489

Majority	..	..	..	427

1892—Jacks (R)	..	..	..	..	..	5296
Noel (LU)	..	..	.:	..	..	4550
Robertson (Lab)	..	..	..	..	..	663

Majority	.. ..	.. ..	746
Liberal Unionist Gain			

Wigtonshire

SIR HERBERT E. MAXW

1895—Unopposed

1892—Sir Herbert Maxwell (C) ..
Coldstream (R) .. .. ..

Majority .. ..
Representation Unchange

Sutherlandshire (See end of S

Elgin and Nairn
MR. J. E. GORDON (C)

1895—J. E. Gordon (C)		2147
J. Seymour Keay (R)		2019
Majority		128
1892—Keay (R)		2533
Gull (LU)		1978
Majority		555

Conservative Gain

Lanarkshire (Govan)
MR. J. WILSON (R)

1895—J. Wilson (R)		4290
G. Ferguson (LU)		4029
Haddow (Lab)		430
Majority		261
1892—Wilson (R)		4829
Spens (C)		3829
Majority		1000

Representation Unchanged

Lanarksh
MR. J. G. HO

1895—J. G. Holborn		
G. A. Whitela		
Ma		
1892—Whitelaw (C)		
Reade (R) ..		
Ma		
R		

Forfarshire
MR. J. MARTIN WHITE (R)

1895—J. M. White (R)		5159
Hon C. M. Ramsay (C)		4718
Majority		441

1892—Rigby (R), 4943 ; Barclay (LU), 4077 :
Majority, 866. Bye-election (November,
1894) — Ramsay (C), 5145 ; Robson (R),
4857 : Majority, 288.

Radical Gain

Lanarkshire (North-East)
MR. G. D. COLVILLE (R)

1895—G. D. Colville (R)		6288
A. Whitelaw (C)		5751
Majority		537
1892—Crawford (R)		5281
Whitelaw (C)		5184
Majority		97

Representation Unchanged

Suth
MR. J. M

1895—J. Macleod (R		
J. A. Swanston		
Maj		
1892—Sutherland (R		
Majority, 846.		
—Macleod Un		
Represen		

IRISH BOROUGHS

Belfast (East

MR. G. W. WOLFF (C)

1895—Unopposed

1892—Unopposed

Representation Unchanged

Belfast (North)

SIR. E. J. HARLAND, BART. (C)

1895—Unopposed

1892—Unopposed

Representation Unchanged

Be

MR. WILLI

18

18

Represe

Belfast (West)

MR. H. O. ARNOLD FORSTER (LU)

1895—Unopposed

1892—Mr. H. O. Arnold Forster (LU)..	..	4266
T. Sexton (AP)	..	3427
Majority	..	839

Representation Unchanged

Cork

MR. MAURICE HEALY (AP)

1895—J. F. X. O'Brien (AP) ..	..	..	..	5327
M. Healy (AP) ..	..	..	..	5169
A. Roche (P) ..	..	..	..	4994
J. C. Blake (P) ..	..	..	..	4966
Majority ..	..	..	..	175

1892—W. O'Brien (AP), 5273; M. Healy (AP),
4759; W. Redmond (P), 3186; Horgan (P),
3077: Majority, 2087. Bye-election (June,
1895)—J. F. X. O'Brien (AP), 4309; Roche
(P), 4132: Majority, 177
Representation Unchanged

MR. J.

1895—J. F. X
M. Hea
A. Roc
J. C. B

1892—W. O'
4759; W
3077: M
1895)—
(P), 41
R

Dublin (College Green)

DR. J. E. KENNY (P)

1895—Unopposed

1892—Kenny (P).. 2568
    Cochrane (C) 1441
    T. D. Sullivan (AP) 1116

      Majority 1127
    Representation Unchanged

Dublin (Harbour)

MR. TIMOTHY HARRINGTON (P)

1895—Unopposed

1892—Harrington (P) 4482
    McDonnell (AP) 1376

      Majority 3106
    Representation Unchanged

Dul

MR. WI

1895—Unopposed

1892—Field (P)
    Murphy (

    Repr

Dublin (St. Stephen's Green)

MR. W. KENNY, Q.C. (LU)

1895—W. Kenny (LU)	3661
Count Plunkett (P)..	3205
Majority	456
1892—Kenny (LU)	2893
Meade (P)..	2878
Pearson (AP)	615
Majority	15
Representation Unchanged	

Galway

MR. J. PINKERTON (AP)

1895—J. Pinkerton (AP)	595
E. Leamy (P)	405
M. Morris (C)	395
Majority	190
1892—Pinkerton (AP)	644
Lynch (P)..	593
Majority	
Representation Unchanged	

MR

1895—P. O'B
J. P. F

18

Limerick City
MR. JOHN DALY (P)

1895—Unopposed

1892—O'Keefe (AP) .. ..
O'Brien (P) .. ..

   Majority .. .. ..
   P Gain from AP

Londonderry City
E. F. VESEY KNOX (A

1895—E. F. V. Knox (AP) .. .. ..
J. Ross, Q.C. (C) .. ..

   Majority .. .. ..

1892—Ross (C) .. ..
McCarthy (AP) .. ..

   Majority .. .. ..
   AP Gain from Conservative

Waterford
MR. JOHN E. REDMOND (P)

1895—J. E. Redmond (P).. 1730
T. G. Farrell (AP).. 1229

   Majority 501

1892—Redmond (P) 1638
Sheehy (AP) 1248

   Majority 390
   Representation Unchanged

Newry
MR. P. G. CARVILL (A

1895—P. G. Carvill (AP).. .. .. ..
H. J. Thomson (C).. .. .. ..

   Majority .. .. ..

1892—Carvill (AP) .. ..
Thomson (C) .. ..
Johnson (P) .. ..

   Majority .. .. ..
   Representation Unchanged

Antrim (East)
CAPTAIN J. M. McCALMONT (C)
1895—Unopposed
1892—Unopposed
Representation Unchanged

Antrim (Mid)
HON. R. T. O'NEILL (C)
1895—Unopposed
1892—Unopposed
Representation Unchanged

Ant
COLONEL HU
1895—Unopposed
1892—Connor (C)
Dodd (R) ..

Maj
Represen

Antrim (South)
MR. W. E. MACARTNEY (C)
1895—Unopposed
1892—Unopposed
Representation Unchanged

Armagh (Mid)
MR. DUNBAR BARTON, Q.C. (C)
1895—Unopposed
1892—Unopposed
Representation Unchanged

A
LIEUT.-COL
1
1
Repre

Armagh (South)

MR. E. M. McHUGH (AP)

1895—E. M. McHugh (AP)	.. ..	378
M. Kavanagh (C)	.. ..	995
	Majority	.. .. ..	1383
1892—McHugh (AP)..	.. ..	3439
Falkiner (C)	.. ..	2242
Blane (P) ..	.. ..	39
	Majority	.. .. ..	1197

Representation Unchanged

Carlow

MR. JOHN HAMMOND (AP)

1895—J. Hammond (AP)	.. ..	3890
S. Duckett (C)..	.. ..	685
	Majority	.. .. ..	3205
1892—Hammond (AP)	.. ..	3738
McMahon (C) ..	.. ..	813
	Majority	.. .. ..	2925

Representation Unchanged

MR. SA

1895—Unoppose

1892—Young (A
Clements

Rep

Cavan (West)
MR. E. F. VESEY KNOX (AP)

1895—Unopposed

1892—Vesey Knox (AP)	6475
Everard (C)	1957
Majority	4518

Representation Unchanged

Clare (East)
MR. WILLIAM REDMOND (P)

1895—W. Redmond (P)	3315
P. McHugh (AP)	3258
Majority	57
1892—Redmond (P)	3314
Cox (AP)	2868
Majority	446

Representation Unchanged

DR.

R

Clar

Cork

Cork (North)

MR. J. C. FLYNN (AP)

1895—Unopposed
1892—Unopposed
Representation Unchanged

Cork (North-East)

MR. W. ABRAHAM (AP)

1895—Unopposed

1892—W. O'Brien (AP), Unopposed.   Bye-election
(June, 1893)—Abraham (AP) Unopposed
Representation Unchanged

MR. EDW

Repre

Cork (South-East)

DR. ANDREW COMMINS (AP)

1895—Unopposed

1892—Morrogh (AP), 4109 ; Shears (C), 692 :
Majority, 3417. Bye-election (1893)—Dr.
Commins (AP) Unopposed

Representation Unchanged

Cork (West)

MR. J. GILHOOLY (AP)

1895—Unopposed					
1892—Gilhooly (AP) ..	..	..	..	..	3155
Payne (LU) ..	..	..	..	..	329
Majority	..	..	..	..	2826

Representation Unchanged

MR. A.

1895—A. O'Conno
E. T. Herd

1892—O'Connor (
Herdman (

Repre

Donegal (North)	Donegal (South)	Don
MR. T. B. CURRAN (AP)	MR. J. G. SWIFT McNEILL (AP)	MR. T. D.

Down (East)
MR. J. A. RENTOUL (C)
1895—Unopposed
1892—Unopposed
Representation Unchanged

Down (North)
LIEUT.-COL. THOMAS WARING (C)
1895—Unopposed
1892—Unopposed
Representation Unchanged

1
MR. M.
1895—M. McCart
T. Rowan (

1
1892—McCartan (
Craig (LU)
Magenis (P

1
Repre

Down (West)

RT. HON. LORD A. HILL (C)

1895—Unopposed
1892—Unopposed
Representation Unchanged

Dublin (North)

MR. J. J. CLANCY (P)

1895—J. J. Clancy (P)	4520
D. Wilson (C)	2280
Majority	2240
1892—Clancy (P)..	3991
Mooney (AP)	2696
Woods (C)..	1638
Majority	1295
Representation Unchanged	

HON.

1895—Hon H
H. Bur

1892—Plunket
French-
Esmond

Re

Fermanagh (North)
MR. R. M. DANE (C)

1895—R. M. Dane (C) 2782
      G. R. Leefer (R) 2406

          Majority 376

1892—Dane (C) 2793
      Jordan (AP) 2483

          Majority 310
      Representation Unchanged

Fermanagh (South)
MR. J. JORDAN (AP)

1895—J. Jordan (AP) 2792
      Sir A. D. Brooke, Bart (C) 2096

          Majority 696

1892—McGittigan (AP) 2941
      Patton (LU) 2320

          Majority 621
      Representation Unchanged

G
MR. J

1895—Unopposed

1892—Roche (AP)
      Lynam (P)

         M
      Repres

Galway, Conn

Galway (North)		Galway (South)		MR. MI

MR. D. KILBRIDE (AP)

1895—D. Kilbride (AP) 2590
Lt-Col J. P. Nolan (P) 2025

Majority 565

1892—Nolan (P) 2040
Tanner (AP) 1651

Majority 389
AP Gain from P

MR. DAVID SHEEHY

1895—Unopposed

1892—Sheehy (AP) 2623
McCarthy (P) 1411

Majority 1212

Representation Unchanged

MR. MI

1895—Unoppos

1892—Sheehan
McGillic

Re

Kerry (North)

MR. THOMAS SEXTON (AP)

1895—Unopposed

1892—Sexton (AP) 2828
    Burke (P) 776
                       ———
        Majority 2052
   Representation Unchanged

Kerry (South)

MR. DENIS KILBRIDE (AP)

1895—Unopposed

1892—Kilbride (AP) 2096
    Foley (P) 225
    Winn (C) 86
                       ———
       Majority 1871
   Representation Unchanged

Ker

SIR THOMAS

1895—Unopposed

1892—Sir Thomas E
    E. Harrington
    Brinsley Fitzg

       Maj
   Represen

Kildare (South)
MR. M. J. MINCH (AP)

1895—Unopposed

1892—Minch (AP) 2642
Leahy (P) 975

Majority 1667

Representation Unchanged

Kilkenny (North)
MR. PATRICK McDERMOTT (AP)

1895—Unopposed

1892—McDermott (AP) 2898
Kavanagh (C) 314

Majority 2584

Representation Unchanged

MR.

1895—Unop

1892—Chan
Majo
1894)

Kildare, North (See end of section)

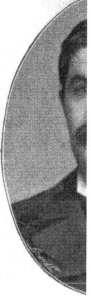

King's County (Birr)

MR. B. C. MOLLOY (AP)

895—Unopposed
892—Molloy (AP) 3329
    Trench (C) 67ʊ
                                   ————
        Majority 2659
Representation Unchanged

King's County (Tullamore)

DR. J. F. FOX (AP)

1895—Unopposed
1892—Unopposed
Representation Unchanged

Lei

MR. PATRICH

1895—Unopposed
18ç2—McHugh (AI
    Tottenham (I

        M:
    Represe

Leitrim (South)
MR. J. TULLY (AP)

1895—Unopposed
1892—Tully (AP) 4271
O'Brien (C) 516
                                    ———
Majority 3755
Representation Unchanged

Limerick (East)
MR. J. FINUCANE (AP)

1895—Unopposed
1892—Finucane (AP).. 2903
Nunan (P).. 1174
                                    ———
Majority 1729
Representation Unchanged

MR. N
1895—Unop
1892—Aus
Har

Londonderry (South)	**Longford (North)**	**Lo**
SIR T. LEA (LU)	MR. JUSTIN McCARTHY (AP)	HON.

195—Sir T. Lea (LU) 4470
Sergeant Dodd (R).. 4060

     Majority 410

192—T. Lea (LU) 4554
Walker (R) 4053

     Majority 501
  Representation Unchanged

1895—Unopposed

1892—McCarthy (AP) 2741
     Wilson (C).. 203

     Majority 2538
  Representation Unchanged

Londonderry, North (See end of section)

1895—Unopposed

1892—Blake (AP)
     Miller (C) .

     N
  Repre

Louth (North)	Louth (South)	
MR. T. M. HEALY (AP)	DR. DANIEL AMBROSE (AP)	MR.

1895—T. M. Healy (AP) 2294
J. Nolan (P) 1433

       Majority 861

1892—Healy (AP) 2268
Callan (Ind. N) 1569

       Majority 699
Representation Unchanged

1895—Dr. D. Ambrose (AP) 2002
J. G. Fitzgerald (P) 1044

       Majority 958

1892—Ambrose (AP) 2451
Nolan (P) 1126

       Majority 1325
Representation Unchanged

1895—Unopp
1892—Dillon
    Fitzgi

Mayo (North)

MR. D. CRILLY (AP)

Meath, South (See end of section)

Mayo (West)

DR. R. AMBROSE (AP)

Mayo, South (See end of section)

Monaghan, North (See end of section)

MR.

Monaghan

Queen's County (Leix)

DR. M. A. MACDONNELL (AP)

1895—Unopposed

1892—MacDonnell (AP) 3261
     Cosby (C) 513
                            ──────
     Majority 2748
   Representation Unchanged

Queen's County (Ossory)

MR. E. CREAN (AP)

1895—E. Crean (AP)
     Colonel H. Poë (C)
     W. A. Macdonald

1892—Crean
     Stop

South)

…DEN (P)

…ority
…ation U…

Sligo (North)

MR. B. COLLERY (AP)

1895—B. Collery (AP)	..	..	..	..	..	3274
H. Harrison (P)	..	..	..	..	..	1281
Sir M. Crofton (C)	..	..	..	..	..	771
Majority		..	..	..	..	1993
1892—Collery (AP)	..	..	..	..	..	4216
Wynn (C)	..	..	..	..	..	..	958
Majority		..	..	..	..	3258

Representation Unchanged

Slig…

MR. THOMAS

895—T. Curran (AP)	..	
— Campbell (C)		
Majori		
1892—Curran (AP)	..	
Ffolliott (C)	..	
Majori		

Representat…

Tipperary (East)

MR. T. J. CONDON (AP)

1895—Unopposed ·

1892—Condon (AP) 2998
Dennehy (P) 891

Majority 2107

Representation Unchanged

Tipperary (Mid)

MR. J. F. HOGAN (AP)

1895—Unopposed

1892—McCarthy (AP), 3284 ; Conway (P), 887 ;
Armstrong (C), 246 ; Majority, 2397. Bye-
election (1893)—J. F. Hogan (AP) Unopposed

Representation Unchanged

Ti

MR. P.

1895—Unopposed

1892—O'Brien (A
Trench (C).

N
Repre

ŀ

Tipperary (South)

MR. J. F. MANDEVILLE (AP)

1895—J. F. Mandeville (AP)		1723
Moore (Ind. N)		1222
	Majority	501
1892—Mandeville (AP)		2571
John O'Connor (P)..		773
	Majority	1798
	Representation Unchanged	

Tyrone (Mid)

MR. G. MURNAGHAN, Q.C. (AP)

1895—G. Murnaghan (AP)		3759
Dr. E. C. Thompson (C)		2252
	Majority	1507
1892—Kenny (AP)		3667
Thompson (C)..		2698
Count Plunkett (P)..		123
	Majority	969
	Representation Unchanged	

Tyrone, East (See end o' section

T

RT. HON. C.

1895—Rt Hon C.		
W. Wilson		
	M	
1892—Hamilton (		
Dougherty		
	M	

Tyrone (South)

MR. T. W. RUSSELL (LU)

1895—T. W. Russell (LU)	..	..	..	..	3239
T. Shillington (R)	..	..	..	..	3046
Majority	..	..	..	..	193
1892—Russell (LU)	..	..	..	..	3468
Dickson (AP)	..	..	..	..	3096
Majority	..	..	..		372

Representation Unchanged

Waterford (East)

MR. P. J. POWER (AP)

1895—Unopposed					
1892—Power (AP)	..	..	..	..	2562
Leamy (P)	..	..	..	..	1042
Majority	..	..	..	1520

Representation Unchanged

MR. ⎱

R⎰

Westmeath (North)	Westmeath (South)	We
MR. J. TUITE (AP)	MR. DONAL SULLIVAN (AP)	MR. THOM

<table>
<tr><td>

1895—Unopposed

1892—Tuite (AP) 2878
    Blaine (P).. 379

         Majority 2499
    Representation Unchanged

</td><td>

1895—Unopposed

1892—Donal Sullivan (AP) 2523
    O'Donoghue (P) 1076

         Majority 1447
    Representation Unchanged

</td><td>

1895—T. J. Healy (
    J. B. Falcon

         M

1892—Healy (AP)
    Magrath (C)

         M
    Represe

</td></tr>
</table>

Wexford (South)

MR. P. FFRENCH (AP)

1895—Unopposed

1892—Barry (AP), 5104 ; Hamilton (C), 354 : Majority, 4750. Bye-election (November, 1893)—Ffrench (AP) returned Unopposed

Representation Unchanged

Wicklow, West (See end of section)

Wicklow (East)

MR. W. J. CORBETT (P)

1895—		
W. J. Corbett (P)	1295
Colonel Tottenham (C)..	1208
E. O'Keeffe (AP)	1077
Majority	87

1892—Sweetman (AP), 1433: Halpin (C), 1195; Corbett (P), 1115 : Majority, 233. Bye-election (April, 1894)—O'Kelly (AP), 1253; Sweetman (P), 1191 ; Tottenham (C), 1165: Majority, 62
P Gain from AP

MAJO

1895—Major
J. Roc

1892—Maguir
O'Conr

CAPTAIN

Repres

Galway (Connemara)
MR. W. O'MALLEY (AP)

1895—Unopposed

| 1892—Foley (AP) | .. | .. | .. | .. | .. | .. | 2637 |
| Joyce (P) | .. | .. | .. | .. | .. | .. | 598 |

| Majority | .. | .. | .. | 2039 |

Representation Unchanged

Kildare (North)
MR. C. J. ENGLEDON (AP)

| 1895—C. J. Engledon (AP) | .. | .. | .. | .. | 1944 |
| J. L. Carew (P) | .. | .. | .. | .. | 1712 |

| Majority | .. | .. | .. | 232 |

| 1892—Kennedy (AP) | .. | .. | .. | .. | 2153 |
| Carew (P) | .. | .. | .. | .. | 1707 |

| Majority | .. | .. | .. | 446 |

Representation Unchanged

Londonderry (North)
RT. HON. J. ATKINSON, Q.C. (C)

| 1895—Rt Hon J. Atkinson (C) | .. | .. | 4763 |
| A. Houston (AP) | .. | .. | .. | 2538 |

| Majority | .. | .. | .. | 2225 |

| 1892—Mulholland (C) | .. | .. | .. | 5490 |
| Green (R) | .. | .. | .. | .. | 2300 |

| Majority | .. | .. | .. | 3190 |

Representation Unchanged

Mayo (South)
MR. MICHAEL DAVITT (AP)

1895—Unopposed

1892—J. F. X. O'Brien (AP) Unopposed

Representation Unchanged

Meath (South)
MR. J. H. PARNELL (P)

| 1895—J. H. Parnell (P) | .. | .. | .. | .. | 2380 |
| J. Jordan (AP) | .. | .. | .. | .. | 2337 |

| Majority | .. | .. | .. | 43 |

1892— Fulham (AP), 2212 ; Dalton (P), 2129 :
Majority, 83. Bye-election (Feb., 1893)—
Jordan (AP), 2707 ; Dalton (P), 2634 :
Majority, 73

P Gain from AP

Monaghan (North)
MR. D. MACALEESE (AP)

| 1895—D. Macaleese (AP) | .. | .. | .. | .. | 3377 |
| Captain the Hon P. C. Westenra (C) | | | 2094 |

| Majority | .. | .. | .. | 1283 |

| 1892—Diamond (AP) | .. | .. | .. | .. | 3697 |
| Jackson (C) | .. | .. | .. | .. | 2230 |

| Majority | .. | .. | .. | 1467 |

Representation Unchanged

Mon
MR. JAI

| 1895—J. Daly (AP) |
| Major W. Te |

| M |

| 1892—O'Driscoll (A |
| Rutherford (|

| M |

Represe

T
MR. P. (

| 1895—P. C. Dugga |
| T. L. Corbe |

| M |

| 1892—Reynolds (A |
| Corbett (C) |

| M |

Repre

W
MR. JAME

1895—Unopposed

| 1892—J. O'Connor |
| Saunders (L |
| J. H. Parnel |

| M |

Repres

NOTE

BLACK AND WHITE *has done all that could be done to make this Parliamentar*
and, considering the brevity of the time available for the collection of portrai
be deemed highly satisfactory. But in certain instances the bustle of the elec
Members from answering the application for their photographs; while in or
may seem, replies have been received to the effect that portraits are not in e
it has been found impossible to furnish a portrait a reference has been inserted
order of the constituencies, and the necessary details have been given at the end of e

The various portraits have been reproduced from excellent likenesses by the follou
who could not, unfortunately, be acknowledged in the usual way under the
in consequence of the form of the volume:

Artistic Portrait Co., Oxford Stree:
Adamson and Son, Rothesay, N.B.
Adkins and Co., Stamford Hill, N.
Austin, G. W., Highbury
Auty and Ruddock, Tynemouth
Adams, W., Reading
Annan and Sons, Glasgow
Asquith, Harrogate

Brown, Barnes and Bell, London and
   Liverpool
Byrne and Co., Richmond, Surrey
Beales and Sons, Spalding
Barrauds, Limited
Baker, Harold, Birmingham
Braithwaite, Leeds

Baum, Franz, Manchester
Browning, Exeter
Hall, Messrs, Waterloo Place, S.W.
Barden, C. H., Chichester
Birtles, Messrs., Warrington
Ball and Co., Peterborough
Boning and Small, Baker Street, W.
Bacon, James and Sons, Leeds
Bacon, James, Northumberland
Bertolli, R. F., March
Brookes, Warwick, Manchester
Bradshaw, G. W., Hastings
Bassano, Old Bond Street, W.
Berlin Studio, Cork

Clarke, J. Palmer, Cambridge

Coles, G., Gloucester
Cobb and Co., Tottenham
Clarke and Co., Maidstone
Chaffin and Sons, Taunton
Coe, Albert E., Norwich
Chapman, H. A., Swansea
Chancellor, Messrs., Dublin
Coles, G., Gloucester
Chalkley, Gould, and Co., Southamp-
   ton
Clark, Bennett, Wolverhampton
Cox, Alfred and Co., Leicester
Crooke, W., Edinburgh
Collier, John, Birmingham
Clarke, Mr., Bury St. Edmunds
Conte, C., Sevenoaks

Creelma
Clare ar

Devereu
Disderi,
Davey,
Debenh
Denny (
Dennie,
Draycot
Debenh
Dickins
Downey
Debenh
Debenh
Debenh

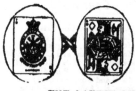

Edwards, John, Hyde Park Corner
Elsden and Son, Hertford
Eastmead, J. J., Rochester
Exley, J., Bradford
Eccles, E., Bury
Elliott and Fry, Baker Street, W.
Ellis, Alfred, Upper Baker Street, W.
Elliott, J. H., Stroud

Fall, T.
Foster, W. F., Bishop's Castle
Fry, W. and A. H., Brighton
Fry, C. E., Gloucester Terrace, S.W.
Fergus, John (Blackdales, Scotland)
Forshaw, W., Oxford
Frankland, J., Blackburn
Fradelle and Young, Regent Street, W.

Glover, M., Dublin
Goldie, J. H., Swansea
Good, A., Crewe
Grossmann, Messrs., Dover
Guy and Co., Cork
Graham, Leamington Spa
Gosney's Studio, Crewkerne Wells
Gauin and Banger, Norwich
Gowland, W. T. and F., York
Gabill and Co., Ebury Street, S.W.
Gregson, Blackburn

Houlton Bros., Trowbridge
Hughes, Alice, Gower Street, W.
Hurst, Stanley, Wrexham
Hayman and Sons, Launceston
Hills and Saunders, Sloane St., S.W.
Hogg, J. Henry, Kendal
Heath, Messrs., Plymouth
Harrison, W. M., Redruth
Henderson and Co., Rochdale
Hawke, John, Plymouth
Harrison and Sons
Howell and Adams, Carmarthen

Hall, G. and J., Wakefield
Harrison, Newcastle, Staffs.
Horsburgh and Sons, London and
  Edinburgh

Illingworth, Halifax

Jakeman and Carver, Hertford
Jerrard, G., Regent Street, W.
Jacobette, Martin, South Kensington
Jones, F. E., Cinderford
Jackson, C. A., Middleton

Keene, Richard, Burton-on-Trent
King, H., Sydney
Kempsell, W. H., Wallington
Kingsbury and Notcutt, Knightsbridge
Kay, E., Bolton

London Photographic Co., Regent St.
Lowthian Bros, Grimsby
Lafosse, Manchester
Lambert, Weston and Son, Folkestone
Lombardi, Pall Mall, East
Lafayette, Dublin, Glasgow, and Man-
  chester
Lawrence, William, Dublin
Lupson, F. and Co., Coventry
Lankester, Percy, S., Tunbridge Wells
Lodge, R. B., Enfield
Leach, B. R., Macclesfield
Laing, J., Shrewsbury
Lavis, C. and R., Eastbourne
London Stereoscopic Co., Regent
  Street, W.
Long, J., Cardiff

Marshall, H., Cambridge Heath, E.
Melhuish, Messrs., Pall Mall
Medrington, Messrs., Liverpool
Moffat, J., Edinburgh
Mc Leish, W., Durham

Midwinter and Co., Bristol
Mavins and Vivash, Belfast
Mc Lanachan, Torquay
Marshall, Wane and Co., Ayr, N.B.
Mendelssohn, H. S., Notting Hill Gate
Mayall and Co., Piccadilly
Maull and Fox, Piccadilly
Moss, E., Ashton-under-Lyne
Monnickindam, Ayr, N.B.
Mowll and Morrison, Liverpool
Magill, James, Belfast

Negretti and Zambra, Crystal Palace
Neame, H., Folkestone

Owen, J., Newtown
Osbourne

Pike, Horace G., Lichfield
Percival, Edgware Road
Pendry, George, Nottingham
Platt Bros., Bolton
Proe, W. S., Peckham
Parker and Co., High Holborn
Page, W., East Grinstead
Phillip and Wright

Robinson and Hinton, Guildford
Ruddock, R. E., Newcastle-on-Tyne
Robinson, Messrs., Dublin
Ralston and Sons, Glasgow
Robinson and Thompson, Birkenhead
Rattie, Kirkcaldy
Russell and Sons, Baker Street, W.

Sawyer, Lyd
Stuart, John, Glasgow
Sachs, Albert, Bradford
Shawcross, Leslie, Blackburn
Soper, T. H., Battersea
Salmon, H. W., Winchester
Sauvy, A., Cork

Stua
Seam
Sims
Scott
Salm
Shaw
Stear
Sma
Spal

Thor
Thon
Turn
Tayl
Turn
Tayl
Trin
Treb
S.

Ushe

Vand
Vale
Vick
Van

Woo
Whit
West
Se
Wen
Wats
Wine
Whi
Will
Whe
Win
Whit
Will
Wils
West
Wal

Lightning Source UK Ltd.
Milton Keynes UK
UKOW05n1440140417
299148UK00001B/13/P